Throw It Don't Hit It

Golf is Easy When You Know How

By

Cec McFarlane

This book is a work of fiction. Places, events, and situations in this story are purely fictional. Any resemblance to actual persons, living or dead, is coincidental.

ISBN: 1-4033-9178-5 (e-book)
ISBN: 1-4033-9179-3 (Paperback)

This book is printed on acid free paper.

1stBooks - rev. 11/08/02

DEDICATION

This book is dedicated to my twin brother

Cedric and his wife Judy

Without their love and support I would not

be who I am today.

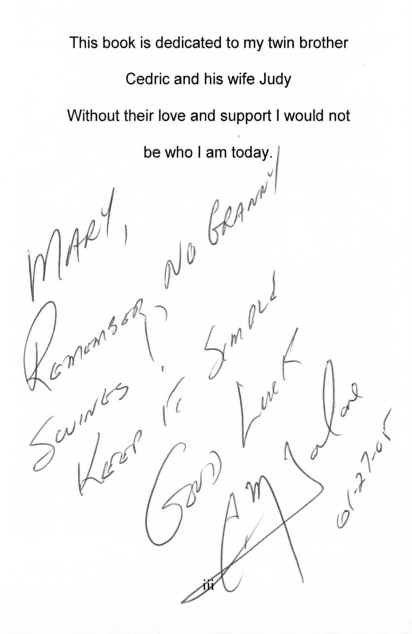

iii

Index

INTRODUCTION ix

CHAPTER 1: THE GOLF STANCE 1

CHAPTER 2: THE GOLF GRIP 7

CHAPTER 3: HOW TO SQUARE UP A CLUB

FACE 13

CHAPTER 4: HOW TO POSITION THE CLUBS

SHAFT 16

CHAPTER 5: HOW TO POSITION THE GOLF

BALL 19

CHAPTER 6: THE GOLF SWING 26

CHAPTER 7: ALIGNMENT 42

CHAPTER 8: HOW TO TAKE THE CLUB BACK

.... 57

CHAPTER 9: PUTTING 63

CHAPTER 10: THE CHIP SHOT 75

CHAPTER 11: THE PITCH SHOT 86

CHAPTER 12: KNOCK DOWN SHOT...............93

CHAPTER 13: SAND PLAY...............................97

CHAPTER 14: TROUBLE SHOTS 107

CHAPTER 15: HITTING WOODS VERSUS

IRONS...115

CHAPTER 16: THE 60% WEDGE...................121

CHAPTER 17: READING BERMUDA GREENS

....127

CHAPTER 18: HOW TO PRACTICE...............134

CHAPTER 19: LESSONS................................142

CHAPTER 20: GOLF CLUBS.........................153

CHAPTER 21: COURSE MANAGEMENT.......165

CHAPTER 22: GOLF ETIQUETTE..................173

CHAPTER 23: ARRIVING AT THE GOLF

COURSE....................................185

CHAPTER 24: GOLF WORDS AND THEIR

MEANINGS 192

CHAPTER 25: SCORE CARDS 202

CHAPTER 26: SWING TRAINING AIDS 214

CHAPTER 27: CONTROLLING THE MENTAL

GAME 218

INTRODUCTION

AS A GOLF TEACHING SPECIALIST , I AM
CONSTANTLY AMAZED AT HOW MOST
TEACHERS AND AMATEURS MAKE THIS
GAME SO DARN DIFFICULT.

UNDERSTANDING THE BASICS OF GOLF
IS SOMETHING THAT VERY FEW PEOPLE
TAKE THE TIME TO DO. THEY ARE SO
WRAPPED UP IN HOW COMPLICATED THE
GAME IS THEY FAIL TO SEE THAT GOLF IS
QUITE SIMPLY A GAME OF ANGLES AND
THAT ONCE YOU UNDERSTAND AND
INCORPORATE THE CORRECT ANGLES A

LARGE PART OF THE GOLF SWING HAPPENS
AUTOMATICALLY.

THIS BOOK HAS BEEN WRITTEN IN AN
EFFORT TO TAKE SOME OF THE SMOKE AND
MIRRORS OUT OF YOUR UNDERSTANDING
OF THE GAME. IF YOU WILL LEARN TO KEEP
THINGS SIMPLE AND ACCEPT THE LAWS OF
PHYSICS YOU WILL BE WELL ON YOUR WAY
TO BECOMING A GOLFER.

ONCE YOU HAVE THE KNOWLEDGE
NECESSARY TO PROMOTE A BASIC GOLF
SWING YOU MUST ALSO LEARN THAT
CHIPPING, PUTTING, PITCHING AND SAND
PLAY ARE SIMPLY SPECIALITY SHOTS AND
THAT THERE IS AN UNIQUE TECHNIQUE FOR

EACH OF THEM. ONCE YOU LEARN THE TECHNIQUES YOU NEED TO PRACTICE THEM IN ORDER TO BECOME EFFICIENT AND EFFECTIVE WITH THEM.

GOLF IS A GAME THAT CANNOT BE SELF TAUGHT, AS YOU CANNOT SEE YOURSELF. MOST AMATEURS ARE EXTREMELY SURPRISED WHEN THEY SEE THEIR SWING ON VIDEO TAPE. THEY FIND IT VERY EYE OPENING AND EDUCATIONAL WHEN THEY SEE WHAT THEY ARE DOING AS OPPOSED TO WHAT THEY THOUGHT THEY WERE DOING. I HAVE HAD NUMEROUS STUDENTS LOOK AT THEIR VIDEO AND RATHER SERIOUSLY RESPOND WITH "I'M NOT DOING THAT". I THEN HAVE HAD TO CONFESS THAT

DURING THE SHORT WALK FROM THE TEACHING AREA TO THE VIDEO VIEWING AREA, I HIRED THEIR TWIN TO DUB OVER THEIR SWING AND MAKE IT LOOK BAD.

MANY PROFESSIONAL TEACHERS ARE GUILTY OF OVER COMPLICATING THEIR GOLF INSTRUCTIONS AND THIS MAKES IT VERY DIFFICULT FOR AMATEURS TO LEARN. THERE IS ALSO A GROUP OF TEACHERS THAT HAVE NEW IDEAS AND THEIR NEW THEORIES ABOUT GOLF WILL MAKE YOU INTO A SCRATCH GOLFER VIRTUALLY OVER NIGHT. YEAH, RIGHT. IT WILL NEVER HAPPEN.. THE AMOUNT OF MIS-INFORMATION AND WRONG INFORMATION IN THE GOLF WORLD IS RAMPANT. SOME

PEOPLE MAKE GOLF SOUND MORE DIFFICULT THAN NUCLEAR SCIENCE (ALL THE SMART PEOPLE ARE GOLFERS AND THE STUPID ONES HAVE TO BECOME NUCLEAR SCIENTISTS) . GOLF IS A GAME CONTROLLED BY PHYSICS AND IT REALLY DOES NOT MATTER HOW YOU HOLD YOUR MOUTH, IF YOU BREAK THE LAWS OF PHYSICS YOU WILL NOT HIT A GOLF BALL CORRECTLY. IT'S AS SIMPLE AS THAT...

MANY AMATEURS ARE HESITANT TO TAKE GOLF LESSONS AS THEY FEAR THEIR SWING WILL BE CHANGED AND THAT THEIR GAME WILL QUICKLY GO DOWN HILL. I HAVE HAD MANY STUDENTS COMPLAIN TO ME THAT THEY CAN NOT DO THE SWING THAT

THEIR TEACHING PRO WANTS THEM TO DO.

THIS IS NOT THE FAULT OF THE STUDENT, IT

IS THE PRO THAT IS WRONG. EACH

STUDENT HAS THEIR OWN UNIQUE SWING

AND THE PROS FUNCTION IS NOT TO

CHANGE IT BUT TO ADJUST THAT SWING TO

THE POINT WHERE THE STUDENT GETS THE

MOST EFFICIENCY AND PRODUCTION OUT

OF IT AS POSSIBLE.

MOST AMATEURS ARE NOT SO NAIVE

THAT THEY BELIEVE THEY ARE GOING TO

SUDDENLY SHOOT PAR GOLF AFTER A FEW

LESSONS. I HAVE FOUND THAT MOST

STUDENTS ARE PLEASED WITH MODERATE

IMPROVEMENT AND MORE IMPORTANTLY,

THAT THEY KNOW WHAT IT IS THEY HAVE TO

WORK ON AND HOW TO WORK ON IT IN ORDER TO IMPROVE THEIR GAME AND GOLF SCORES.

TEACHING PROS ARE WELL PAID FOR THEIR EXPERTISE AND IT IS THEIR RESPONSIBILITY THAT THEIR STUDENTS RECEIVE EXCEPTIONAL VALUE FOR THEIR EXPENDITURES. I DO NOT BELIEVE AMATEURS WANT INSTRUCTION TO BE CANDY COATED, COMPLICATED OR DIFFICULT TO DO. THEY NEED STRAIGHT FORWARD HONEST INSTRUCTION THAT WILL HELP THEM IMPROVE.

I HOPE THAT THE INFORMATION CONTAINED WITHIN THIS BOOK WILL ASSIST YOU IN PERFECTING AN IMPERFECT GAME.

CHAPTER 1

THE GOLF STANCE

THE GOLF STANCE

THIS IS ONE OF THE SIMPLEST THINGS IN GOLF TO DO YET IT REMAINS A PROBLEM FOR A LOT OF AMATEURS.

QUITE SIMPLY THE GOLF STANCE IS NOTHING MORE OR LESS THAN THE ATHLETIC STANCE. TO LEARN IT HERE IS AN EASY WAY. STAND UP AND HAVE ONE OF YOUR FRIENDS PRETEND THAT THEY HAVE A BASKETBALL AND THE NET IS BEHIND YOU. YOUR JOB IS TO GUARD THE NET AND KEEP YOUR FRIEND FROM SCORING. ONCE YOU LOOSEN UP AND GO WITH THE GAME

YOU WILL FIND THAT DURING YOUR GUARDING OF THE NET AND STOPPING YOUR FRIEND FROM SCORING YOU WILL HAVE....WIDENED YOUR STANCE TO WHERE YOUR FEET ARE JUST ABOUT UNDER YOUR ARM PITS...YOU HAVE A SLIGHT KNEE FLEX THAT IS ALLOWING YOU TO MOVE EASILY IN ANY DIRECTION...YOU HAVE TILTED YOUR BACK SLIGHTLY FORWARD AND YOUR ARMS ARE OUT TO YOUR SIDES, SIMILAR TO THAT OF A GUN FIGHTER GETTING READY TO DRAW....AND YOUR BODY IS FAIRLY RELAXED......NOW TAKE YOUR ARMS AND WITHOUT BENDING THEM PUT YOUR HANDS TOGETHER ABOUT A FIST FROM THE FRONT OF YOUR PELVIC AREA...AND STAY

LOOSE.....THAT IS THE GOLF STANCE. I.E. THE ATHLETIC STANCE.

THE REASON FOR YOUR HANDS BEING ONE FIST FROM YOUR PELVIC AREA IS FOR BALANCE. IF THEY ARE FURTHER AWAY FROM YOUR BODY, DUE TO YOUR SHOULDER BLADES BEING THE HEAVIEST PART OF YOUR UPPER BODY, YOU WILL BE OFF BALANCE WHEN YOU TRY AND DO THE GOLF SWING. IF YOU HAVE POOR BALANCE YOUR COMPUTER WILL MAKE ADJUSTMENTS DURING YOUR GOLF SWING THAT YOU WILL HAVE NO CONTROL OVER . IF YOU ARE TOP HEAVY YOUR COMPUTER WILL MAKE YOU LIFT YOUR BODY DURING THE GOLF SWING TO AVOID YOU FALLING

ON YOUR FACE. THIS WILL RESULT IN A POOR SWING AND VERY POOR BALL STRIKING.

A LOT OF TIMES DURING YOUR GOLF OUTINGS YOU HAVE HEARD SOMEONE TELL ANOTHER PERSON THAT THEY HAVE LIFTED THEIR HEAD. WELL 99 TIMES OUT OF 100 THEY HAVE NOT LIFTED THEIR HEAD THEIR COMPUTER HAS LIFTED THEIR WHOLE BODY TO COMPENSATE FOR A SWING OR STANCE FLAW.

FOR THOSE OF YOU WONDERING WHAT THE COMPUTER IS...IT IS SIMPLY YOUR BRAIN AND IT CONTROLS EVERYTHING AND EVERY MOVE THAT YOU MAKE. IT IS THE

SINGLE MOST IMPORTANT THING IN GOLF

AND BELIEVE ME IT WILL MAKE

ADJUSTMENTS OVER WHICH YOU HAVE

ABSOLUTELY NO CONTROL....IT CANNOT BE

FOOLED...AT LEAST NOT BY YOU...

PRACTICE YOUR GOLF STANCE IN FRONT

OF SLIDING GLASS DOORS OR A MIRROR

AND MAKE SURE YOU ARE RELAXED .

CHAPTER 2

THE GOLF GRIP

Cec McFarlane

THE GOLF GRIP

HERE I AM GOING TO INTRODUCE YOU TO A NEW WORD AN EXTREMELY IMPORTANT NEW WORD, AND THAT WORD IS "SQUARE". YOU WILL FIND THAT EVERYTHING IN GOLF IS RELATED TO BEING SQUARE OR IN OTHER WORDS HAVING THE CORRECT ANGLES.

THE GOLF GRIP STARTS WITH THE CLUB BEING POSITIONED CORRECTLY IN THE LEFT HAND (LEFTIES YOU KNOW EVERYTHING IS OPPOSITE). THE BUTT OF A GOLF CLUB IS SLIGHTLY CONTOURED SO

THAT THE END OF THE GRIP FLARES A LITTLE . MAKE SURE YOU DO NOT GRIP A CLUB AT THE VERY END. LEAVE THE FLARED PART A LITTLE ABOVE YOUR HAND. THE GOLF CLUB FITS IN THE LEFT HAND FROM THE MEAT OF YOUR PALM AND ACROSS THE THICKEST JOINT OF YOUR FORE FINGER. DO NOT, I REPEAT DO NOT, HOLD THE CLUB IN THE FINGERS ONLY AS THIS WILL ALLOW LITTLE CONTROL OF THE CLUB HEAD. CLOSE YOUR LEFT HAND OVER THE CLUB WITH YOUR THUMB POINTING STRAIGHT DOWN THE FRONT OF THE SHAFT. WHEN HELD PROPERLY YOU SHOULD BE ABLE TO REMOVE YOUR THUMB AND FOREFINGER, HOLDING THE CLUB WITH ONLY THE BACK THREE FINGERS AND STILL FEEL AS IF YOU

HAVE FULL CONTROL OVER IT. THE ONLY
PRESSURE ON THE SHAFT, FROM THE LEFT
HAND, SHOULD BE THESE THREE FINGERS,
THE THUMB AND FOREFINGER SHOULD BE
HELD VERY LIGHTLY ON THE SHAFT.

NOW FOR THE RIGHT HAND (AGAIN
LEFTIES YOU KNOW THE DIFFERENCE) YOU
HAVE THREE ACCEPTABLE OPTIONS WITH
YOUR RIGHT HAND. YOU CAN HOLD THE
CLUB WITH ALL YOUR FINGERS ON THE
SHAFT OR YOU CAN HAVE YOUR FRONT
THREE FINGERS ON THE SHAFT AND
INTERLOCK YOUR LITTLE FINGER WITH
YOUR LEFT FOREFINGER OR YOU CAN HAVE
YOUR FRONT THREE FINGERS ON THE
SHAFT AND OVER LAP YOUR RIGHT LITTLE

FINGER OVER YOUR LEFT FOREFINGER. ANY OF THESE GRIPS ARE ACCEPTABLE AND THE ONE YOU ELECT TO USE IS YOUR CHOICE. THE SHAFT SHOULD BE PLACED AND HELD GENTLY IN THE SECOND JOINT OF YOUR RIGHT HAND FINGERS. YOUR TWO HANDS SHOULD BE MARRIED TOGETHER WITH THE MEATY PART OF THE RIGHT PALM FITTING INTO THE DEPRESSION OF THE THUMB OF THE LEFT HAND. YOUR RIGHT THUMB SHOULD BE PLACED TO THE LEFT OF THE SHAFT AND NEVER STRAIGHT DOWN THE SHAFT AS THAT WILL HINDER PROPER WRIST MOVEMENT DURING THE SWING.

THE BACK OF THE LEFT HAND SHOULD BE LINED UP TO THE TARGET LINE (I.E.

SQUARE) AND THE BACK OF THE RIGHT HAND SHOULD BE EXACTLY OPPOSITE, POINTING AWAY FROM THE TARGET LINE. THIS WILL GIVE YOU A NEUTRAL OR SQUARE GRIP AND WILL GREATLY ENHANCE YOUR CHANCES AT ACHIEVING PROPER CLUB AND HAND ACTION THROUGH THE HITTING ZONE.

THE PRESSURE OF YOUR GRIP SHOULD BE THAT OF HOLDING A BABY BIRD, YOU DO NOT WANT IT TO FLY AWAY BUT YOU ALSO DO NOT WANT TO CHOKE THE LITTLE FELLOW. STAY LOOSE AS TIGHTNESS PROMOTES NOTHING BUT PROBLEMS FOR A GOLF SWING....LOOSE AS A GOOSE!!!

CHAPTER 3

HOW TO SQUARE UP A

CLUB FACE

HOW TO SQUARE UP A CLUB FACE

IN ORDER FOR A GOLF BALL TO GO IN A STRAIGHT LINE IT IS IMPERATIVE THAT THE CLUB FACE BE SQUARE AT IMPACT.

YOU LINE A CLUB FACE UP BY HAVING THE BOTTOM OF THE FACE COME STRAIGHT BACK TOWARDS THE MIDDLE OF YOUR STANCE. DO NOT TRY TO LINE A CLUB UP WITH THE TOP OF IT OR IT WILL BE CLOSED.

LET THE CLUB SETTLE ON THE GROUND BY ITSELF, DO NOT MANIPULATE IT, AS IT IS

MANUFACTURED TO AUTOMATICALLY SQUARE ITSELF UP.

REMEMBER ITS THE BOTTOM EDGE AND NOT THE TOP EDGE THAT SQUARES A CLUB FACE.

CHAPTER 4

HOW TO POSITION THE

CLUBS SHAFT

<u>**HOW TO POSITION THE CLUBS SHAFT**</u>

IF YOU LET A GOLF CLUB SIT NATURAL IT WILL POINT TO THE LEFT CENTER OF YOUR GROIN. (THE OPPOSITE FOR YOU LEFTIES)

THIS WILL AUTOMATICALLY PLACE YOUR HANDS IF FRONT OF THE GOLF BALL. HANDS IN FRONT OF THE BALL IS A VERY ABUSED AND MISUNDERSTOOD PART OF GOLF. IF ANY PART OF YOUR FORWARD HAND IS IN FRONT OF THE GOLF BALL (AS IT WILL BE IF YOU LET A CLUB SIT NATURAL) THEN YOUR HANDS ARE ACTUALLY IN FRONT OF THE BALL. DO NOT MAKE THE MISTAKE OF

17

FORWARD PRESSING YOUR HANDS IN AN ATTEMPT TO PUT THEM IN A POSITION THAT YOU HAVE MISUNDERSTOOD, AS THIS WILL CLOSE THE CLUB FACE AND CHANGE THE LOFT OF THE CLUB. THIS CAN LEAD TO MANY PROBLEMS IN YOUR GOLF SWING AND BALL FLIGHT.

CHAPTER 5

HOW TO POSITION THE

GOLF BALL

HOW TO POSITION THE GOLF BALL

I SHUDDER TO THINK OF THE THOUSANDS OF TIMES I HAVE SEEN IMPROPER POSITIONING OF THE GOLF BALL. AMATEURS ARE TOLD (BY PROS THAT SHOULD BE TEACHING TENNIS AND NOT GOLF) TO MOVE THE BALL FORWARD FOR THEIR WOODS AND BACK FOR THEIR IRONS. THIS GIVES AN INCORRECT UNDERSTANDING OF WHERE THE GOLF BALL SHOULD BE PLAYED AS MOST AMATEURS PLAY IT WAY TO FAR FORWARD IN THEIR STANCE TO BE SOLID BALL STRIKERS.

THINK OF HOW YOU LINE UP TO A GOLF BALL AND THE STANCE THAT YOU TAKE. YOU HAVE CREATED A TRIANGLE WITH THE BOTTOM PORTION OF YOUR BODY AND AS SOON AS YOU PUT YOUR HANDS TOGETHER YOU HAVE NOW CREATED ANOTHER TRIANGLE WITH THE TOP HALF OF YOUR BODY. NOW YOU ARE IN A POSITION TO DO A PENDULUM SWING, THUS YOU HAVE BECOME A HUMAN PENDULUM. WHEN YOU MAKE A GOLF SWING THE CLUB HEAD WILL BOTTOM OUT AT THE BOTTOM OF THE PENDULUM AND YOU WANT TO STRIKE THE BALL AS THE CLUB PASSES THE BOTTOM AND STARTS ITS UPWARD MOTION.

IF YOU PLAY THE GOLF BALL WAY UP OFF YOUR LEFT HEAL YOU WILL HAVE TO DO SOME SORT OF A WEIRD MOVE WITH YOUR BODY TO REACH IT AND THAT IS NOT WHAT WE WANT TO DO TO OUR GOLF SWING AS YOU WANT TO BE ACCELERATING TOWARD THE TARGET AS YOU COME THROUGH THE BALL AND NOT LEANING BACK TO REACH A BALL THAT IS TOO FAR FORWARD IN YOUR STANCE.

THE POSITION OF THE GOLF BALL IS AN ILLUSION THAT IT IS WAY FORWARD IN YOUR STANCE, IT IS ACTUALLY PLAYED FROM JUST FORWARD OF CENTER ON ALL FULL SHOTS.

HERE IS HOW IT IS ACCOMPLISHED: WHEN YOU LINE UP TO A GOLF BALL PUT IT SLIGHTLY FORWARD OF THE CENTER OF YOUR BODY AND HAVE BOTH YOUR FEET TOGETHER. NOW IF YOU HAVE A SHORT IRON IN YOUR HANDS TAKE A SMALL STEP FORWARD WITH YOUR LEFT FOOT AND A SMALL STEP BACK WITH YOUR RIGHT. (LEFTIES REMEMBER IT IS OPPOSITE) . IT WILL NOW BE EVIDENT THAT THE GOLF BALL IS SLIGHTLY FORWARD OF THE CENTER OF YOUR PENDULUM AND YOU WILL STRIKE IT AS THE CLUB STARTS UP IN THE FORWARD SWING. GREAT THAT'S HOW IT SHOULD BE.....NOW FOR THE ILLUSION PART.... WITH A WOOD IN YOUR HANDS AGAIN LINE UP TO THE BALL WITH IT JUST SLIGHTLY FORWARD

OF THE CENTER OF YOUR BODY AND HAVE BOTH FEET TOGETHER.. NOW TAKE A SMALL STEP FORWARD WITH YOUR LEFT FOOT AND A LARGE STEP BACK WITH YOUR RIGHT FOOT. IT WILL LOOK AS IF THE BALL IS BEING PLAYED OFF YOUR LEFT HEEL BUT YOU CAN READILY TELL THAT IT IS STILL IN REALITY JUST FORWARD OF THE CENTER OF YOUR BODY, WHERE IT BELONGS AND WHERE IT NEEDS TO BE IF YOU ARE GOING TO MAKE SOLID CONTACT AND ACCELERATE TOWARDS THE TARGET.

IF YOU WATCH THE PROS YOU WILL SEE THAT THEY PLAY THE BALL FROM THIS JUST FORWARD OF CENTER POSITION EVEN IF THEY DON'T UNDERSTAND PHYSICS AND

24

THINK THE ILLUSION IS THE ACTUAL BALL POSITION.

REMEMBER GOLF IS A GAME OF ANGLES AND IF YOU WANT SOLID BALL STRIKING YOU HAD BETTER PAY ATTENTION TO THIS ONE.

CHAPTER 6

THE GOLF SWING

<u>**THE GOLF SWING**</u>

THERE HAVE BEEN COUNTLESS THEORIES REGARDING THE GOLF SWING. YOU HEAR OF EVERYTHING FROM GRAVITY GOLF, NATURAL GOLF, THE 36 STEP GOLF SWING TO SONIC GOLF, PLUS THERE ARE A MULTITUDE OF CLUBS ON THE MARKET THAT WILL PRODUCE THE PERFECT SWING. OTHER THAN MAKING THE INVENTORS OF THESE AMAZING GIMMICKS A TON OF MONEY, THEY DO NOT, HAVE NOT, WILL NOT AND CAN NOT PRODUCE THE PERFECT GOLF SWING. THE REASON IS RATHER SIMPLE....THERE IS NO SUCH BEAST..

EVERY GOLFER HAS THEIR OWN UNIQUE SWING, THAT IS CAUSED BY MANY FACTORS SUCH AS AGE, AGILITY, STRENGTH, ATHLETIC ABILITY, HEIGHT, PHYSICAL CONDITION ETC. ETC. ETC.....

EVEN THOUGH ALL SWINGS ARE DIFFERENT THERE ARE CERTAIN POSITIONS THAT YOU MUST TRY AND OBTAIN IF YOU ARE TO PRODUCE THE BEST GOLF SWING THAT YOU AS AN INDIVIDUAL CAN DO. YOU MUST HAVE A GOLF SWING THAT CONFORMS TO CERTAIN LAWS OF NATURE AND PHYSICS IF YOU EXPECT TO BE CONSISTENT AND BE ABLE TO ENJOY THIS WONDERFUL SPORT.

THE GOLF SWING IS ACTUALLY A VERY SIMPLISTIC CONCEPT...YOU DON'T HIT AT A GOLF BALL YOU THROW IT WITH AN UNDERHAND MOTION....THAT CERTAINLY GOT YOUR ATTENTION .

IF YOU WANT TO EXPERIENCE THE FEELING OF DOING A GOLF SWING HERE IS WHAT YOU NEED TO DO. TAKE YOUR GOLF STANCE WITHOUT A CLUB, HOLD YOUR HANDS TOGETHER IN FRONT OF YOUR BODY AS IF YOU WERE ACTUALLY HOLDING A CLUB. NOW TAKE A GOLF BALL IN YOUR RIGHT HAND (LEFTIES REMEMBER EVERYTHING IS ALWAYS THE OPPOSITE FOR YOU) . NOW DROP YOUR LEFT HAND TO

THE SIDE OF YOUR BODY AND SIMPLY LIFT THE RIGHT ARM INTO THAT OF A THROWING POSITION (PICTURE A WAITER HOLDING A TRAY OR SIMPLY SAYING "HOW"). MAKE SURE THAT YOU DO NOT TURN YOUR BODY, SIMPLY LIFT THE RIGHT ARM INTO THE TRAY POSITION. NOW, UNDERHAND, THROW THE GOLF BALL AND LET YOUR WHOLE BODY MOVE FORWARD WITH THE MOVE. YOU WILL FIND THAT YOU WILL FINISH WITH YOUR RIGHT ARM EXTENDED HIGH AND TOWARD THE TARGET AND BY HAVING LET YOUR BODY MOVE WITH THE THROW YOUR WEIGHT WILL HAVE AUTOMATICALLY SHIFTED FORWARD. YOUR RIGHT FOOT WILL HAVE BEEN DRAGGED OFF THE

GROUND WITH THE TOE NOW POINTING STRAIGHT DOWN.

YOU HAVE NOW JUST MADE AND FELT A GOLF SWING. YOU WILL FIND THAT IT TAKES PRACTICE TO THROW A BALL UNDERHAND WHEN BOTH HANDS ARE INVOLVED AS MOST AMATEURS WANT TO HIT THE BALL AND THAT CAUSES THEIR INITIAL MOVEMENT FORWARD TO BE DONE WITH THEIR ARMS ONLY. TO DO A GOLF SWING OR THROWING OF THE BALL, EVERYTHING MOVES FORWARD AT THE SAME TIME. YOU OFTEN HEAR THE LESS KNOWLEDGEABLE

GOLF TEACHERS TALK ABOUT THE LOWER PART OF THE BODY, SUCH AS THE HIPS BEING THROWN FORWARD, AS BEING

31

THE INITIAL MOVE IN THE FORWARD GOLF SWING. YOU CAN PROVE THIS THEORY IS INCORRECT BY SIMPLY TRYING TO DO THE ONE HANDED UNDERHAND THROW BY THROWING YOUR HIPS FORWARD BEFORE YOU DO THE ACTUAL THROW...BE CAREFUL AS IT WILL BE NOT ONLY BE AWKWARD TO DO IT WILL BE VIRTUALLY IMPOSSIBLE TO DO WITH ANY RHYTHM. WHEN YOU THROW A BALL UNDERHANDED EVERYTHING HAPPENS IN SUCH A CO-ORDINATED MANNER THAT IT IS IMPOSSIBLE TO TELL WHAT PART OF THE HUMAN BODY MOVES FIRST, IT ALL JUST HAPPENS.

THERE IS ANOTHER WIDELY MISUNDERSTOOD PART OF THE GOLF

SWING AND THAT IS THE SO CALLED TURNING OF THE HIPS DURING THE BACK SWING. THERE IS ACTUALLY VERY LITTLE HIP TURN WHEN THE PROPER BACK SWING IS DONE.

HERE IS AN EXERCISE THAT YOU CAN DO TO HELP YOU UNDERSTAND THE HIPS AND THEIR FUNCTION DURING THE BACK SWING. THIS TIME TAKE YOUR GOLF STANCE WITH AN IRON IN YOUR HANDS. REMOVE YOUR LEFT HAND FROM THE CLUB AND LET IT GO DOWN TO YOUR SIDE. NOW SIMPLY LIFT THE CLUB WITH YOUR RIGHT ARM TO THE TRAY OR THROWING POSITION. DO NOT TURN YOUR BODY OR LET YOUR HIPS TURN. KEEP YOUR BELT BUCKLE FACING AS FORWARD

AS YOU CAN. WITHOUT LETTING YOUR BODY OR HIPS TURN REACH UP AND GRAB THE SHAFT OF THE IRON WITH YOUR LEFT HAND.. YOU WILL IMMEDIATELY FEEL VERY TIGHT AND COILED WITH A LOT OF COILING PRESSURE IN YOUR SIDES. THAT IS WHAT A PROPER BACK SWING FEELS LIKE.....IT IS A "COIL" NOT A TURN....THIS COILED POSITION IS WHAT ALLOWS YOU TO BECOME A HUMAN SPRING AND GIVES YOU TREMENDOUS POWER. ONCE YOU HAVE ALLOWED YOUR HIPS TO TURN IN THE BACK SWING YOU HAVE LOST ALL POWER (EXCEPT FOR YOUR ARMS) AND THE GOLF CLUB HAS BEEN TAKEN OFF LINE.

TO PROVE TO YOURSELF THAT THE BACK SWING IN GOLF IS ACTUALLY A COILING MOVEMENT, DO THIS FOLLOWING EXERCISE. TAKE YOUR GOLF STANCE WITH A GOLF CLUB IN YOUR HANDS, REMOVE YOUR LEFT HAND FROM THE CLUB AND LIFT THE CLUB INTO THE THROWING POSITION OR TRAY POSITION KEEPING YOUR HIPS FIRM. NOW GARB THE SHAFT OF THE CLUB WITH YOUR LEFT HAND BUT ALLOW YOUR HIPS TO ROTATE BACK AWAY FROM THE BALL POSITION. YOU WILL NOW NOTICE THAT YOU HAVE LOST THE COILED FEELING AND IT WILL BE VIRTUALLY IMPOSSIBLE TO THROW THE CLUB FORWARD BY AN UNDERHAND TYPE OF A MOVEMENT AS YOUR UPPER BODY IS NOW TURNED

COMPLETELY AWAY FROM THE YOUR LINE TO THE TARGET. THE ONLY WAY YOU CAN MAKE THE GOLF CLUB MOVE FORWARD FROM THIS POSITION IS TO INITIATE THE MOVE WITH YOUR ARMS . THIS IS ONE OF THE THINGS THAT CAUSE AN OVER THE TOP OR CASTING MOVEMENT IN YOUR GOLF SWING. IF YOU WERE TO THROW A BALL UNDERHANDED IN THIS MANNER THE OTHER GUYS WOULD MAKE YOU PLAY FOR THE GIRLS TEAM..

NOW THAT YOU HAVE MASTERED THE BACK PORTION OF A GOLF SWING (YEAH.....RIGHT.....) LETS DISCUSS THE FORWARD FINISH. WHEN YOU THREW THE BALL WITH ONE HAND, REMEMBER HOW

YOUR WEIGHT SHIFTED AUTOMATICALLY
AND YOU FINISHED HIGH WITH YOUR RIGHT
TOE POINTING STRAIGHT DOWN.. THIS IS
THE POSITION THAT YOU NEED TO
DUPLICATE WHEN YOU HAVE BOTH HANDS
ON THE CLUB AND YOU THROW THEM
FORWARD. WITH BOTH HANDS ON THE CLUB
DO A PRACTICE SWING MAKING SURE YOUR
HANDS FINISH VERY HIGH. HOLD THAT
FINISH AND YOU WILL NOTICE THAT YOUR
LEFT ARM IS NOW IN A TRAY HOLDING
POSITION AND YOUR RIGHT TOE IS
POINTING STRAIGHT DOWN. THIS WILL LOOK
VERY PRETTY SO LET'S CALL IT A PRETTY
TRAY FINISH. THUS IF YOU FINISH YOUR
GOLF SWING AND EITHER YOUR ARMS ARE
NOT HIGH OR YOUR RIGHT TOE IS NOT

POINTING STRAIGHT DOWN, IT WILL NOT BE
PRETTY. TO GET TO THIS PRETTY TRAY
FINISH YOU WILL NOTICE THAT YOU HAVE
TO ACCELERATE THE FORWARD SWING IN
ORDER TO GET YOUR BODY AND ARMS IN
THE CORRECT POSITION.

AT THIS STAGE YOU SHOULD BE ABLE TO
COMPLETE AN ENTIRE GOLF SWING WITH
EASE. LET'S GO THROUGH A COMPLETE
SWING FROM YOUR INITIAL STANCE TO THE
COMPLETION OF THE SWING. TAKE YOUR
ATHLETIC STANCE AND LINE UP TO THE
GOLF BALL. MAKE SURE YOU FEEL VERY
COMFORTABLE AND THAT THERE IS NO
TENSION IN ANY PART OF YOUR BODY.
HAVE THE BUTT OF THE IRON

APPROXIMATELY ONE FIST AWAY FROM YOUR GROIN. NOW LIFT THE CLUB (WITH BOTH HANDS) INTO THE TRAY POSITION , BE VERY CAREFUL NOT TO LIFT IT UP TOO STEEP. (TO AVOID THIS TENDENCY MAKE SURE YOUR LEFT ARM IS FAIRLY STRAIGHT OR JUST SLIGHTLY BENT BUT DEFINITELY NOT IN A LOCKED POSITION , THIS WILL KEEP THE GOLF CLUB AWAY FROM YOUR BODY AND ALLOW YOU TO ATTAIN THE TRAY POSITION AT THE TOP OF YOUR BACK SWING). BE SURE THAT YOUR HIPS AND BELT BUCKLE HAVE STAYED AS FIRM AS YOU CAN KEEP THEM AND THAT YOU FEEL COILED AT THE TOP OF THE BACK SWING. NOW, UNDERHANDED, THROW EVERYTHING THAT YOU OWN FORWARD IN THE

DIRECTION OF THE TARGET LETTING YOUR ENTIRE BODY RELEASE AND GO FORWARD WITH THE MOMENTUM OF THE THROW. YOU SHOULD AUTOMATICALLY FINISHED WITH YOUR ARMS HIGH TO THE TARGET AND THE RESULTING WEIGHT SHIFT HAS CAUSED YOUR RIGHT FOOT TO HAVE LEFT THE GROUND WITH THE TOE POINTING STRAIGHT DOWN. YOU SHOULD ALMOST FEEL THAT YOU COULD CONTINUE YOUR FORWARD MOVEMENT AND ACTUALLY START WALKING TO THE TARGET AS YOUR WEIGHT HAS SHIFTED SO FAR FORWARD. IF YOU WANT TO SEE A SUCCESSFUL PRO THAT REALLY DEMONSTRATES THIS MOVE, WATCH GARY PLAYER SWING, HE ACTUALLY

DOES START WALKING TOWARD THE TARGET AS HE COMPLETES HIS SWING.

THE GOLF SWING GOES UP TO UP......BASEBALL IS AROUND AND AROUND...

DOING THE PROPER GOLF SWING MAKES EVERYTHING FEEL VERY EFFORTLESS...AS IT SHOULD BE.

REMEMBER THROW A GOLF BALL FROM A COILED POSITION , NEVER HIT A GOLF BALL...THERE IS NO HIT IN GOLF...IT IS A SWING OR IN OTHER WORDS...A THROWING MOTION.

CHAPTER 7

ALIGNMENT

ALIGNMENT

THERE IS NOTHING MORE CRITICAL TO THE GOLF SWING THAN ALIGNMENT. IT'S BY FAR THE MOST ABUSED AND MISUNDERSTOOD PART OF GOLF.

HOW IMPORTANT IS ALIGNMENT.....WELL A LOT OF WORLD CLASS PROS HAVE THEIR CADDIES STAND BEHIND THEM TO LINE THEM UP PROPERLY AS A GOLF TOURING PROFESSIONAL REALIZES THAT IT IS PHYSICALLY IMPOSSIBLE TO DO A CORRECT GOLF SWING IF THEY ARE NOT ALIGNED SQUARE TO THE TARGET LINE.

ALIGNMENT IS SO IMPORTANT BECAUSE OUR COMPUTER (BRAIN) WILL DO THINGS TO OUR SWING THAT WE HAVE NO CONTROL OVER IF WE ARE NOT ALIGNED CORRECTLY. THE COMPUTER SIMPLY WANTS TO SEND THE BALL TO WHERE WE TOLD IT WE WANT IT TO GO.

IF WE LINE UP TO THE RIGHT OF THE TARGET LINE OUR COMPUTER WILL FORCE OUR MUSCLES TO GO OVER THE TOP AS IT IS TRYING TO PULL THE BALL BACK TO THE TARGET WE THOUGHT WE WERE LINED UP TO. IF WE LINE UP TO THE LEFT THE COMPUTER WILL MAKE THE MUSCLES PUSH THE BALL BACK TO THE INSTRUCTED

TARGET LINE. BOTH OF THESE SITUATIONS CAN CAUSE THINGS SUCH AS SLICES, DUCK HOOKS, FAT SHOTS, THIN SHOTS AND TOPPING OF THE BALL AND WE HAVE ABSOLUTELY NO CONTROL OVER SAME AS WE WERE THE ONE WHO GAVE OUR COMPUTER AN INSTRUCTION AND THEN PROCEEDED TO LINE UP IN A WAY THAT MADE IT NEARLY IMPOSSIBLE TO COMPLETE. IT HAS DONE ITS BEST, AND SO WHAT OUR BALL STRIKING WAS TERRIBLE, IT WAS ONLY TRYING TO MAKE US HAPPY.

YOU HAVE ALL HEARD SOME HIGH HANDICAP GOLFER WHINE ABOUT HAVING A PERFECT PRACTICE SWING AND THEN BEING UNABLE TO HIT THE GOLF BALL. THE

NEXT TIME YOU HAVE THE HONOR OF HEARING THIS COMPLAINT WATCH THIS GOLFERS ALIGNMENT ON THEIR NEXT SHOT AND YOU WILL SEE THAT THEY ARE LINED UP 10 - 30 YARDS RIGHT OF THE TARGET. WHEN THEY MAKE THEIR PERFECT PRACTICE SWING THE COMPUTER ALLOWS IT AS THERE IS NO CONCRETE TARGET IN MIND. HOWEVER AS SOON AS THIS GOLFER IS READY TO MAKE A SWING AT AN ACTUAL TARGET AND LINES UP TO THE RIGHT THE COMPUTER WILL STEP IN AND FORCE THE MUSCLES TO PULL THE BALL BACK IN AN EFFORT TO GET THE BALL TO IT'S INSTRUCTED TARGET..

THIS SAME GOLFER WILL OCCASIONALLY SEE A PRO AND BE SHOWN THE BASICS OF LINING UP CORRECTLY, AFTER A DOZEN OR SO TERRIBLE SWINGS HE WILL USUALLY SAY WELL THAT'S NOT MY PROBLEM AND THEN CONTINUE ON TO WHINE ANOTHER DAY. WHAT AN AMATEUR FAILS TO OR WILL NOT ACCEPT IS THAT THE OVER THE TOP SWING HAS BEEN CAUSED BY YEARS OF BAD ALIGNMENT AND THEIR BAD SWING ANGLE HAS BECOME A HABIT.....GUESS WHAT....YOU ARE NOT GOING TO BREAK A BAD HABIT IN ONE EASY LESSON. IT WILL TAKE TIME, EFFORT AND PATIENCE AS YOU MUST CREATE A NEW HABIT IN ORDER TO BREAK OR REPLACE AN OLD ONE. JUST THINK IF SOMEONE WERE TO TRY AND

TEACH YOU TO WALK DIFFERENT THAN YOU DO, IT WILL TAKE TIME AS HOW YOU WALK IS A HABIT. WHEN YOU WORK ON CORRECTING YOUR ALIGNMENT, REMEMBER THAT IT IS YOUR COMPUTER TRYING TO OVER COME THE HABITS OF YOUR MUSCLES (MUSCLE MEMORY)....THE COMPUTER WILL WIN AS IN MOST PEOPLE MUSCLES HAVE VERY LITTLE INTELLIGENCE, THEY ARE JUST STUBBORN....

ALIGNMENT IS A PROBLEM TO ALL GOLFERS AS WE HAVE ONE STRONG EYE AND ONE WEAK EYE. THIS VISION FLAW MAKES IT IMPOSSIBLE TO STAND SIDEWAYS AND ALIGN CORRECTLY AS EACH EYE IS SEEING A DIFFERENT ANGLE AND THE

COMPUTER CANNOT ADJUST TO WHICH ONE IS SENDING IT THE CORRECT MESSAGE. MOST GOLFERS LINE THEIR BODY UP TO THE TARGET AND THAT WOULD BE NICE IF IT WERE THEIR BODY THAT THEY ARE TRYING TO THROW TO THE TARGET. THINK OF THE PROVERBIAL RAILWAY TRACK SYSTEM, THE BALL AND CLUB FACE ARE ON ONE TRACK GOING IN A STRAIGHT LINE TO THE TARGET, THE GOLF CLUB IS THE TRESTLE AND YOU ARE HOLDING THE END OF IT THE FURTHEST FROM THE BALL AND CLUB HEAD....GUESS WHAT TRESTLES DO, THEY SUPPORT TWO TRACKS, SO IF THE BALL AND CLUB HEAD ARE ON ONE AND YOU ARE HOLDING THE OPPOSITE END, YOU MUST BE STANDING ON THE PARALLEL

TRACK. OR IN A STRAIGHT LINE DIRECTLY
BESIDE THE OTHER TRACK. (ALSO KNOWN
AS BEING SQUARE TO THE LINE) . IF YOU
WERE TO PUT YOUR BODY ON THE SAME
TRACK AS THE BALL AND CLUB HEAD YOU
WOULD HAVE TO HOLD THE TRESTLE
STRAIGHT UP IN THE AIR AND THIS WOULD
MAKE IT RATHER DIFFICULT TO SWING
WITHOUT BREAKING YOUR OWN ANKLES. IF
YOU LINE YOUR BODY TO THE OTHER
TRACK AND WANT TO EXTEND THE TRESTLE
(CLUB) IT WILL NOW BE AIMED TOO FAR TO
THE RIGHT AND GUESS WHAT....HERE
COMES THAT OLD COMPUTER AND WILL
PULL OR THROW THE CLUB OVER THE TOP
TO TRY AND GET THE BALL BACK TO WHERE
IT BELONGS....AND THERE IS NOTHING IN

THE WORLD THAT YOU CAN DO TO STOP IT....UNLESS OF COURSE YOU DECIDE TO LINE UP CORRECTLY.

TO CORRECT THE ALIGNMENT PROBLEM, WHEN YOU PRACTICE LAY A CLUB DOWN POINTING APPROXIMATELY 5 YARDS LEFT OF YOUR BALL TARGET AND MAKE SURE IT IS BETWEEN YOU AND THE BALL WHEN YOU TAKE YOUR STANCE. IT IS CRITICAL THAT THIS CLUB (WE CALL IT A CHEATER CLUB) DOES NOT POINT AT THE BALL TARGET OR YOU WILL BE CORRECTING NOTHING. YOU CANNOT PLACE THIS CLUB DOWN AND EXPECT IT TO BE CORRECT FROM YOUR STANCE POSITION, REMEMBER THE EYE PROBLEM, WHAT YOU MUST DO IS WALK 10 -

20 FEET BEHIND IT ONCE YOU HAVE IT IN POSITION AND YOU WILL THEN AND ONLY THEN BE ABLE TO SEE WHERE IT IS ACTUALLY POINTING. THIS IS CRITICAL AS IF YOU DON'T DO IT YOU ARE WASTING YOUR TIME. WHEN YOU LINE UP MAKE SURE YOUR BOTH FEET ARE PARALLEL TO THE CHEATER CLUB. YOU WILL FEEL AS IF YOU ARE AIMING WAY LEFT OF THE TARGET AND GUESS WHAT, YOU ARE!!!, HOWEVER IT IS NOT YOU GOING TO THE TARGET IT IS THE GOLF BALL AND IF YOU ARE LEFT IT IS ON LINE. WHEN YOU SWING THINK OF THROWING EVERYTHING TO THE BALL TARGET. YOU WILL IN THE BEGINNING ONLY HIT 2 OR 3 BALLS OUT OF 10 THAT ARE RELATIVELY STRAIGHT AND THE REST

COULD GO ANYWHERE. ACCEPT THE FACT THAT YOU WILL HAVE TO TOLERATE THIS FRUSTRATION IF YOU EVER WANT TO CORRECT THE WORSE PROBLEM IN GOLF. YOU WILL SOON START TO HIT 5 OR 6 BALLS OUT OF 10 REASONABLY STRAIGHT AND AS THIS OCCURS YOU WILL HAVE THE FEELING THAT IT IS SO MUCH EASIER TO SWING THROUGH THE BALL AND YOU ARE USING A LOT LESS EFFORT TO STRIKE THE BALL . YOU WILL ALSO GAIN FROM 7 TO 15 EXTRA YARDS WITH EACH CLUB ONCE YOU CORRECT AN OVER THE TOP SWING. THE REASON FOR THIS IS SIMPLE, AN OVER THE TOP SWING IS ALL ARMS WHERE AS THE CORRECT SWING INCORPORATES THE

ENTIRE BODY AND THE POWER THAT
WEIGHT SHIFTING CAN ADD TO A SWING.

WHEN YOU PLAY, PICK A TARGET
APPROXIMATELY 5 YARDS TO THE LEFT OF
YOUR BALL TARGET AND LINE YOUR BODY
UP TO IT. THE LENGTH OF THE CLUB WILL
DETERMINE HOW FAR IT WILL ACTUALLY
MOVE YOUR BODY LEFT OF THE TARGET IN
ORDER TO CREATE CORRECT ALIGNMENT.
ALTHOUGH YOU WILL DEFINITELY FEEL
THAT YOU ARE TOO FAR LEFT....TRUST IT
AND SWING EVERYTHING YOU OWN TO THE
BALL TARGET. REMEMBER DON'T HIT AT THE
BALL, THROW IT UNDERHANDED TO THE
TARGET.(SEE CHAPTER 6, THE GOLF SWING)

YOU MOST LIKELY HAVE HEARD SOME PEOPLE SAY THAT THEY PICK A SPOT A FEW FEET OR YARDS IN FRONT OF THEIR BALL TO HELP THEM LINE UP. I GUARANTEE YOU THEY WILL NOT BE ABLE TO LINE UP CORRECTLY. JUST THINK THAT IF YOU WERE TO JUMP IN YOUR CAR AND HEAD DOWN THE ROAD AT 70 MILES AN HOUR LOOKING AT A SPOT JUST IN FRONT OF YOUR HOOD, YOU KNOW WHAT WOULD HAPPEN....YEP...ONE BIG CRASH.!! LETS NOT CRASH IN GOLF AND THEREFORE PICK YOUR TARGET PAST YOUR BALL TARGET...THIS WILL ALLOW THE COMPUTER TO HELP DEFEAT THOSE STUPID STUBBORN MUSCLES THAT ARE TRYING TO DRIVE YOU TO DRINK...OR IN IT...

THE SECRET TO ALIGNMENT....THERE ARE TWO TARGETS IN GOLF....THE BALL TARGET....AND THE IMPORTANT OR "BODY" TARGET. LEARN TO LINE UP CORRECTLY AND PRACTICE UNTIL YOU ERASE OLD MUSCLE MEMORY AND YOUR GOLF SWING WILL DRASTICALLY IMPROVE AS WELL AS YOUR BALL STRIKING..

CHAPTER 8

HOW TO TAKE THE CLUB

BACK

<u>HOW TO TAKE THE CLUB BACK</u>

ONCE YOU HAVE LEARNED ALIGNMENT, IT IS CRITICAL THAT THE GOLF CLUB BE TAKEN AWAY FROM THE BALL AT THE CORRECT ANGLE OR YOU WILL NEVER ATTAIN ACCURACY IN YOUR GOLF SHOTS.

THE CLUB IS LIFTED AWAY FROM THE BALL, IT IS NOT TURNED AWAY.

YOU HEAR PROS TALK ABOUT THE CLUB BEING TAKEN AWAY FROM THE BALL ON A SLIGHTLY INSIDE PATH. MOST AMATEURS ATTEMPT THIS BY TURNING THE CLUB AWAY

OR TRYING TO MAKE SURE THEY TAKE IT INSIDE. THIS IS ONE OF THE WORST MOVES THAT YOU CAN MAKE AS IT WILL AUTOMATICALLY MAKE THE CLUB GO OFF YOUR INTENDED LINE AND YOU WILL BE VERY LUCKY TO RETURN IT TO SQUARE THROUGH THE BALL. YES, EVERY ONCE IN A WHILE YOU WILL SQUARE THE CLUB THROUGH THE BALL IF YOUR SWING HAS THIS FLAW....HOWEVER ALL THAT PROVES IS THAT A BROKEN WATCH IS RIGHT TWICE A DAY..

BECAUSE YOUR HANDS ARE A DIFFERENT LENGTH ON THE CLUB. I.E. ONE IS ABOVE THE OTHER. IF YOU SIMPLY TAKE THE CLUB BACK IN WHAT YOU MENTALLY

THINK IS A STRAIGHT LINE IT WILL AUTOMATICALLY GO SLIGHTLY INSIDE . THAT IS NOT A SECRET TO GOLF IT IS SIMPLE PHYSICS.

DO NOT MAKE THIS GAME ANY MORE DIFFICULT THAN YOU HAVE TO....THERE ARE MANY PARTS OF THIS GAME THAT OCCUR AUTOMATICALLY DUE TO PHYSICS ETC.

TO MAKE SURE YOU ARE TAKING THE CLUB BACK AT THE PROPER ANGLE, LIFT IT HALF WAY UP IN BACK (TO YOUR HIPS) AND CHECK THE ANGLE OF THE TOE OF THE CLUB. IF YOU HAVE DONE IT PROPER THE TOE WILL BE POINTING STRAIGHT UP IN THE

AIR . IF IT IS NOT YOU HAVE MADE AN INCORRECT TAKE AWAY OF THE GOLF CLUB.

YOU CAN ALSO CHECK YOUR FORWARD ANGLE BY SWINGING THE CLUB TOWARDS THE TARGET AND AGAIN STOPPING HALF WAY UP . LOOK AT THE TOE OF THE CLUB AND IF IT IS NOT POINTING STRAIGHT UP IN THE AIR YOU HAVE A SWING PROBLEM THAT NEEDS TO BE CORRECTED.

A GOOD EXERCISE TO TRY AND TEACH YOURSELF THE PROPER SWING ANGLES IS TO HIT BALLS WITH A HALF SWING TRYING TO MAKE SURE YOUR CLUB GOES TOE UP IN BACK TO TOE UP IN FRONT. DO NOT TRY TO

POWER THE GOLF BALL, JUST DO THE SWING AND YOU WILL KNOW WHEN YOU HAVE DONE IT CORRECTLY BECAUSE THE BALL WILL GO OFF THE FACE OF THE CLUB A LOT EASIER AND WITH MORE ZEST THAN YOU HAVE FELT BEFORE.

IF YOU HAVE A SWING FLAW YOU CANNOT DO THE TOE UP TO TOE UP EXERCISE PROPERLY......ALSO IF YOU DO NOT HAVE PROPER ALIGNMENT THIS EXERCISE CANNOT BE DONE CORRECTLY.....DARN....THERE'S THAT WORD AGAIN....."ALIGNMENT" ......GOLFERS BEST FRIEND OR WORSE ENEMY.......YOUR CHOICE......

CHAPTER 9

PUTTING

PUTTING

PUTTING IS AN ART THAT IS REQUIRED TO BE LEARNED. MOST AMATEURS OVERLOOK THIS PORTION OF THEIR GOLF GAME AND THEY USUALLY FEEL THEY ARE GOOD PUTTERS. IF THEY WERE EVER TO KEEP STATISTICS ON THEIR PUTTING THEY WOULD BE SURPRISED AT HOW MANY STROKES THEY AVERAGE PER ROUND. THE BEST PROS AND LEADING MONEY WINNERS ON THE PGA ARE ALL EXCEPTIONAL PUTTERS AND THEY WORK EXTREMELY HARD TO KEEP THEIR PUTTING SKILLS FINELY TUNED.

THE TYPE OF PUTTER, HOW YOU STAND, HOW YOU HOLD THE PUTTER AND THE SIZE OF THE PUTTER HEAD ARE ALL PERSONAL CHOICES AND ARE LEFT SOLELY TO EACH INDIVIDUAL PLAYER.

IF THE TRUTH WERE TO BE KNOWN, IT IS NOT THE COST OF A PUTTER THAT MAKES IT THE RIGHT ONE FOR YOU. IT IS HOW IT FEELS AND LOOKS TO YOU THAT IS IMPORTANT. I HAVE SEEN SOME EXTREMELY GOOD PUTTERS THAT USED K-MART SPECIALS AND I HAVE SEEN EVEN MORE TERRIBLE PUTTERS THAT USE $200 PUTTERS. IN PUTTING IT IS USUALLY THE FAULT OF THE RIDER AND NOT THE HORSE.

THERE ARE 5 RULES IN PUTTING THAT YOU CANNOT BREAK OR YOU WILL NEVER HAVE A CHANCE OF BEING KNOWN AS OR BE A GREAT PUTTER.

1/ YOU MUST BE SQUARE TO YOUR TARGET LINE. (DARN, THERE YOU GO AGAIN WITH THAT STUPID ALIGNMENT THING) OR YOU WILL HAVE A TENDENCY TO PUSH OR PULL YOUR PUTTS.

2/ YOUR EYES MUST BE DIRECTLY OVER THE GOLF BALL. YOU CAN CHECK THIS BY TAKING YOUR STANCE OVER A PUTT AND HAVING A BUDDY HOLD A BALL AT THE TIP OF YOUR NOSE AND THEN LET IT DROP

STRAIGHT DOWN. IF IT HITS THE BALL YOU ARE LINED UP TO THEN YOUR EYES ARE OVER THE BALL. OTHERWISE YOU NEED TO CORRECT YOUR STANCE UNTIL THEY ARE. UNLESS YOUR EYES SEE THE SAME ANGLE TO THE HOLE AS YOUR BALL WILL BE TRAVELING YOU ARE LEAVING YOURSELF OPEN TO MISSED PUTTS.

3/ YOU MUST DO A PENDULUM STROKE. I.E. YOUR HANDS, WRISTS, ARMS AND SHOULDERS ARE ALL MOVED AS A ONE PIECE UNIT. THERE CAN BE NO FLIPPING OR BREAKING OF THE WRISTS DURING A PUTT. YOU ARE SIMPLY A HUMAN PENDULUM. REMEMBER A PENDULUM GOES BACK AND FORTH IN A STRAIGHT LINE AND DOESN'T

STOP IN THE MIDDLE OF ITS FORWARD SWING, IN OTHER WORDS YOU MUST FOLLOW THROUGH TO THE TARGET WHEN MAKING A PUTTING STROKE.

4/ NEVER THINK ABOUT HOW HARD TO HIT A PUTT.........WHAT.....THIS PRO MUST BE ON DRUGS!!! BEFORE YOU CALL IN THE MEN IN THE WHITE SUITS TO TAKE ME AWAY, LET ME EXPLAIN. MAKING A PUTTING STROKE IS LIKE THROWING A BALL TO THE HOLE. TO PROVE THIS, LINE UP A COUPLE OF PUTTS OF SAY 20 FEET. PUTT THE FIRST ONE IN YOUR NORMAL MANNER. NOW ON THE SECOND ONE LINE UP OVER THE BALL, WHEN YOU ARE READY, LOOK AT THE HOLE AND VISUALIZE ROLLING THE BALL UP TO IT,

NOW LOOK SLOWLY BACK TO YOUR BALL AND CLOSE YOUR EYES AND MAKE THE PUTT. YOU SHOULD BE SURPRISED AS TO HOW THE BALL WITH YOUR EYES CLOSED REACTED AND HOW NICE IT ROLLED TO THE HOLE. YOU HAVE JUST LET YOUR COMPUTER ALLOW YOU TO THROW A BALL TO THE HOLE. HERE IS ANOTHER EXERCISE TO TRY, TAKE TWO GOLF BALLS AND PICK TWO HOLES DIFFERENT DISTANCES FROM YOU, NOW TOSS EACH BALL UNDERHAND TO EACH OF THE HOLES. I GUARANTEE YOU THAT YOU DIDN'T THINK OF HOW FAR TO TAKE EACH BALL BACK OR HOW MUCH OF A FOLLOW THROUGH TO MAKE. YOU SIMPLY THREW THE BALLS TO THE HOLES. WELL, THAT IS ALL THAT PUTTING TRULY IS. IF YOU

EVER FIND YOURSELF TRYING TO DECIDE HOW HARD TO HIT A PUTT, BACK OFF AND LET YOUR COMPUTER DO ITS JOB. IT WILL BE ABLE TO JUDGE DISTANCE AND THE POWER IT TAKES TO GET THERE FAR BETTER THAN YOU WILL EVER BE ABLE TO.

5/ NEVER HIT A PUTT THAT BREAKS......SEE MYRTLE, I TOLD YOU THIS PRO WAS ON SOMETHING......WELL MAYBE YOU WILL CHANGE YOUR MIND AFTER YOU READ THE FOLLOWING. IT IS MUCH EASIER TO HIT A STRAIGHT PUTT THAN A PUTT THAT BREAKS, SO LETS TAKE THE BREAK OUT OF THE PUTTING STROKE. WHEN YOU ARE LINING UP YOUR PUTT AND YOU ARE DOWN LOW BEHIND THE GOLF BALL LOOKING FOR

THE CONTOURS OF THE GREEN, IMAGINE THIS. YOU HAVE THROWN A BUCKET OF WATER BETWEEN YOUR BALL AND THE HOLE AND YOU ARE GOING TO WATCH AND SEE WHAT THE WATER DOES. IF IT FLOWS TO THE RIGHT YOUR BALL WILL BREAK TO THE RIGHT. IF IT FLOWS QUICKLY TO THE RIGHT YOUR BALL WILL HAVE MORE BREAK TO IT. NOW THAT YOU HAVE DONE THIS YOU WILL HAVE AN IDEA OF APPROXIMATELY HOW FAR THE BALL WILL BREAK. NOW, HERE IS HOW WE HIT A STRAIGHT PUTT. IF YOU FEEL THAT THE BALL WILL BREAK 3 INCHES TO THE RIGHT I WANT YOU TO BUILD AN IMAGINARY HOLE 3 INCHES TO THE LEFT OF THE REAL HOLE. IF YOU PUTT IN A STRAIGHT LINE TO THE NEW

IMAGINARY HOLE THAT YOU HAVE CREATED
YOU WILL HAVE SUCCEEDED IN MAKING A
BREAKING PUTT INTO A STRAIGHT PUTT,
AND IF YOUR ASSESSMENT OF THE BREAK
IS CORRECT YOU HAVE A GOOD CHANCE AT
MAKING THE PUTT.

HERE IS THE FINAL SECRET TO
BECOMING A GREAT PUTTER. WHEN YOU
PRACTICE AND HAVE BUILT YOUR
IMAGINARY HOLE, ACTUALLY PLACE A
COLORED GOLF BALL IN THAT SPOT AND
WHEN YOU PLAY YOUR COMPUTER WILL
RELATE TO THAT IMAGE. WE ARE NOT DONE
YET, AS ONLY A DARN FOOL WOULD EVER
TRY TO HIT A GOLF BALL INTO A HOLE AS
SMALL AS THE ONES ON THE GREEN. WELL

LET'S MAKE IT BIGGER. AGAIN WHEN YOU PRACTICE AND HAVE PUT A COLORED BALL IN THE SPOT OF YOUR NEW IMAGINED HOLE TAKE 4 OR 5 MORE COLORED BALLS AND PLACE THEM IN A TWO FOOT CIRCLE AROUND THE HOLE. THAT IS NOW THE SIZE OF THE GOLF HOLE THAT YOU WANT TO BE PUTTING TO. IT IS SURE A LOT EASIER IN YOUR MIND TO GET A BALL CLOSE TO A TWO FOOT CIRCLE THAN A VERY SMALL CUP. PRACTICE THROWING YOUR PUTTS TO THIS NEW HOLE AND THE SIZE OF IT AND YOU WILL BE SURPRISED AT HOW MANY PUTTS BECOME SIMPLE TAP INS. YOU ARE ALLOWED TWO PUTTS PER HOLE IF YOU WANT TO SHOOT PAR GOLF. IF THIS METHOD KNOCKS OFF 3 OR 4 STROKES YOU

HAVE NOW GAINED ON YOUR GOLF SCORE. AND AS USUAL WHEN YOU ARE ON THE COURSE YOU WILL ACTUALLY SEE THESE COLORED BALLS AROUND THE HOLE AND THEY WILL ASSIST YOU.

IF YOU PRACTICE THE 5 RULES YOUR PUTTING WILL IMPROVE AND ONCE YOUR PUTTING IMPROVES SO WILL YOUR SHORT GAME. A GOOD PUTTER AUTOMATICALLY BECOMES A GOOD SHORT GAME PLAYER BECAUSE THE PRESSURE OF HAVING TO GET THE BALL SO CLOSE TO THE HOLE IS OFF AND IT WILL LET YOU MAKE MORE CONSISTENT CHIP AND PITCH SHOTS.

CHAPTER 10

THE CHIP SHOT

THE CHIP SHOT

THE CHIP SHOT IS ONE OF THE SPECIALITY SHOTS THAT REQUIRES THE PROPER TECHNIQUE IN ORDER TO BE SUCCESSFUL.

CHIPPING IS SIMPLY AN ADAPTED FORM OF PUTTING, WHERE AS THE WRISTS DO NOT BREAK IN THE FORWARD PART OF THE STROKE.

FOR SHORT CHIP SHOTS, PLAY THE BALL BACK IN YOUR STANCE, KEEP YOUR HANDS FORWARD, AND HAVE APPROXIMATELY 60%

OF YOUR WEIGHT FORWARD. STROKE THE BALL WITH A PUTTING STROKE. I.E. A PENDULUM MOTION MAKING SURE THAT YOU DO NOT ATTEMPT TO LIFT THE BALL INTO THE AIR BY LETTING YOUR WRISTS BREAK OR FLIP THROUGH THE BALL. THE STROKE SHOULD BE FIRM WITH AN ACCELERATION TOWARDS THE TARGET. AS IN PUTTING, DO NOT ATTEMPT TO FIGURE OUT HOW HARD TO HIT THE BALL....LET THE COMPUTER DO IT.

FOR LONGER CHIPS, PLAY THE BALL THE SAME WAY IN YOUR STANCE, HANDS , WEIGHT ETC. THIS SHOT REQUIRES A MODIFIED STROKE DUE TO ITS DISTANCE REQUIREMENT. THE MODIFICATION IS THAT

THE BACK SWING IS ALLOWED TO BE LIFTED INTO THE AIR AND YOUR WRISTS SHOULD HINGE. YOU NOW STROKE THROUGH THE BALL MAKING SURE YOUR WRISTS DO NOT BREAK IN THE FORWARD PART OF YOUR STROKE, THEY STAY FIRM AS IN A PUTT. AGAIN LET THE COMPUTER DO IT JOB.

AMATEURS USUALLY CHOOSE THE WRONG CLUB FOR THEIR CHIPS. THEY SEE A TOURING PRO DO AN AMAZING FLOP SHOT AND IMMEDIATELY THEY TRY AND IMITATE IT. AMATEURS NEITHER HAVE THE ABILITY OR KNOWLEDGE TO COMPLETE THE FLOP SHOT ON A CONSISTENT BASIS. THIS SHOT IS ONE OF THE LOWEST PERCENTAGE SHOTS IN ALL OF GOLF AND EVEN THE

PROS (WITH A COUPLE OF EXCEPTIONS) USE IT ONLY WHEN ABSOLUTELY NECESSARY. THE FLOP SHOT LOOKS PRETTY BUT IT LEAVES TOO MUCH ROOM FOR AN ERROR TO BE MADE. A RECENT EXAMPLE OF THE RISK OF THIS SHOT WAS SHOWN BY THE GREAT TIGER WOODS AT THE 2002 BUICK OPEN. ON THE PAR 3 17TH HOLE TIGER PUSHED HIS TEE SHOT SHORT AND RIGHT OF THE GREEN. HE HAD ABOUT A 30 YARD SHOT TO THE PIN OVER THE EDGE OF A BUNKER. HE ELECTED TO DO THE FLOP SHOT AND SIMPLY BLEW IT. THE GOLF BALL FLEW 10 YARDS PAST THE HOLE AND ENDED UP IN A GREEN SIDE BUNKER. HE THEN HIT HIS SAND SHOT (HIS 3RD SHOT) ABOUT 12 FEET PAST THE PIN AND MISSED

HIS COME BACK PUTT FOR A NASTY LITTLE 5 ON HIS SCORE CARD. HE DID NOT EVEN WAIT UNTIL HIS PLAYING PARTNER FINISHED HIS PUTT, HE STRODE OFF THE GREEN IN A HUFF AND WENT MUTTERING TO THE NEXT TEE. IF THE BEST IN THE WORLD CAN MISS THIS SHOT, WHY IN THE WORLD WOULD AN AMATEUR EVEN CONSIDER IT UNLESS ALL OTHER OPTIONS ARE IMPOSSIBLE. IN OTHER WORDS, BE VERY CAREFUL ABOUT USING THE FLOP SHOT....YOU WILL FIND THE CHIP SHOT IS MUCH SAFER AND THE BALL WILL HAVE PLENTY OF HEIGHT WHEN REQUIRED.

HOW YOU PICK THE CLUB THAT IS REQUIRED FOR THE CHIP SHOT IS RATHER

SIMPLE. WHENEVER YOU ARE FACED WITH A CHIP SHOT, THINK OF HOW YOU WOULD THROW A BALL UNDERHANDED TO GET IT TO THE PIN. THIS WILL DETERMINE THE CORRECT CLUB TO USE FOR THAT PARTICULAR CHIP SHOT. IF A LOW TRAJECTORY WILL GET THE BALL TO THE HOLE, CHIP WITH A 7 IRON WHERE AS IF YOU NEED A HIGHER TRAJECTORY TO CLEAR AN OBJECT, A 8 - 9 OR WEDGE MAY BE REQUIRED. IF YOU WANT TO SCORE IN GOLF YOU HAVE TO LEARN THAT THE LOWER THE FLIGHT OF THE GOLF BALL AROUND THE GREEN THE GREATER YOUR ODDS ARE OF MAKING THE SHOT.

NOW THAT YOU KNOW TO IMAGINE TOSSING THE BALL UNDERHANDED TO THE HOLE YOU NEED TO LEARN JUST HOW MUCH LOFT EACH OF YOUR GOLF CLUBS HAVE AND HOW THEY WILL REACT TO BOTH THE SHORT AND LONG CHIP SHOT. FOR EXAMPLE: A SAND WEDGE WILL CHIP VERY HIGH AND ROLL VERY LITTLE WHERE A 7 IRON WILL CHIP LOWER AND ROLL A LOT MORE. YOU NEED TO PRACTICE WITH ALL OF YOUR CLUBS UNTIL YOU CAN AUTOMATICALLY DECIDE WHICH CLUB WILL PRODUCE THE SAME FLIGHT OF THE GOLF BALL AS YOU DETERMINED WAS REQUIRED BY THE UNDER HAND THROW PRE-SHOT ROUTINE.

HERE IS A LITTLE EXERCISE TO TEACH YOU A BIT ABOUT HOW YOUR CLUBS HAVE FAR MORE LOFT TO THEM THAN YOU USUALLY REALIZE. FIND AN OBJECT THAT IS APPROXIMATELY 3 FEET HIGH THAT IS BETWEEN YOU AND A FLAG. NOW PLACE A BALL ON THE GROUND APPROXIMATELY 10 FEET FROM THE OBJECT AND KEEPING THAT OBJECT DIRECTLY BETWEEN YOUR BALL AND THE FLAG. NOW TAKE A 7 IRON AND DO A CHIP SHOT. DO NOT ATTEMPT TO LIFT THE BALL OR ASSIST IT INTO THE AIR, SIMPLY DO AN ACCELERATED CHIP SHOT WITH YOUR WRISTS STAYING FIRM. IF YOU DO THE CHIP SHOT CORRECTLY THE BALL WILL CLEAR THE OBJECT WITH A COUPLE OF FEET TO SPARE. IF YOU CANNOT CLEAR

THIS OBJECT YOU NEED A LOT OF PRACTICE WITH THE CHIP SHOT.

ONCE YOU CAN CLEAR AN OBJECT SUCH AS THE ONE ABOVE YOU WILL COME TO REALIZE THAT YOU HAVE BEEN USING WAY TOO MUCH LOFT ON THE CLUBS YOU HAVE BEEN CHIPPING WITH. THIS IS THE FIRST STEP TO YOUR BECOMING A GOOD CHIPPER.

THE CHIP SHOT HAS NO WRIST BREAK AND THAT MAKES THE BALL HAVE OVER SPIN OR IN OTHER WORDS IT WILL TRACK TO THE HOLE. ONCE YOU BREAK YOUR WRISTS THE BALL WILL HAVE BACK SPIN

AND A TENDENCY TO CHECK UP OR STOP

ONCE IT LANDS.

CHAPTER 11

THE PITCH SHOT

THE PITCH SHOT

THE PITCH SHOT IS A SPECIALITY SHOT WHERE THE BALL GOES HIGH AND HAS A LOT OF SPIN ON IT SO THAT IT WILL STOP OR CHECK UP QUICKLY ONCE THE BALL LANDS ON THE GREEN. THE PITCH SHOT IS PLAYED WITH THE BALL FORWARD IN YOUR STANCE, HANDS ARE FORWARD AND APPROXIMATELY 60% OF YOUR WEIGHT IS FORWARD. THE CLUB IS LIFTED AT A FAIRLY STEEP ANGLE TO ONLY 3/4 OF A NORMAL BACK SWING. YOU THEN HIT DOWN HARD ON THE GOLF BALL AND ACCELERATE TO A 3/4 FINISH.

WHEN DONE CORRECTLY THE GOLF CLUB WILL STRIKE THE GOLF BALL ON A DOWNWARD PATH AND THE BALL WILL FEEL AS IF IT HAS JUMPED OFF THE FACE. THIS SHOT IMPARTS TREMENDOUS BACK SPIN ON A GOLF BALL.

YOU WILL NEED TO PRACTICE THIS SHOT WITH YOUR SHORT IRONS AND WEDGES TO SEE HOW EACH OF THEM WILL REACT.

ONCE YOU HAVE MASTERED THE PITCH SHOT YOU CAN NOW HAVE SOME FUN WITH CONTROLLED DISTANCES AND SPIN.

AS AN EXAMPLE: TAKE A NINE IRON AND DO A NORMAL PITCH SHOT WITH IT AND NOTE HOW THE BALL HAS REACTED TO DISTANCE AND SPIN. NOW TAKE THE SAME CLUB AND CHOKE DOWN A COUPLE OF INCHES ON THE SHAFT AND MAKE THE SAME SWING. YOU SHOULD NOTICE THAT THE BALL HAS REACTED ALMOST IDENTICAL TO THE PREVIOUS SWING WITH THE EXCEPTION THAT IT HAS FLOWN A MUCH SHORTER DISTANCE. NOW TAKE THE SAME CLUB AND OPEN THE FACE OF IT A FEW DEGREES AND MAKE THE SAME SWING (NOTE: WHEN YOU OPEN THE FACE OF A CLUB YOU MUST ADJUST YOUR STANCE TO A MORE OPEN POSITION AS THE CLUB FACE CHANGES THE DIRECTION OF WHERE IT IS

AIMING) . YOU WILL NOTICE THAT WITH THIS OPEN FACE THE BALL WILL GO MUCH HIGHER AND SHORTER BUT WILL STILL HAVE THAT JUMP OFF THE FACE OF THE CLUB FEELING.

EXPERIMENT WITH DIFFERENT CLUBS BY CHOKING DOWN ON THEM TO VARIED LENGTHS AND OPENING THE FACE TO A VARIETY OF DEGREES AND YOU WILL SOON COME TO REALIZE THAT YOU CAN REALLY VARY THE HEIGHT AND DISTANCE OF ANY SHORT IRON OR WEDGE, WHILE MAINTAINING THE REQUIRED BACK SPIN TO MAKE THE BALL CHECK ON A GREEN. MOST PROS CAN TAKE A NINE IRON AND BY CHOKING WAY DOWN ON THE SHAFT AND

OPENING THE CLUB FACE WIDE OPEN, HIT AN ACCELERATED GOLF SHOT THAT WILL GO NO FURTHER THAN 10 - 12 FEET AND STOP ON A DIME. WITH PRACTICE YOU WILL BE AMAZED AT HOW WELL YOU WILL BE ABLE TO CONTROL YOUR CLUBS INSTEAD OF THEM CONTROLLING YOU.

THE SECRET TO THE PITCH SHOT IS TO HIT DOWN HARD AND THROUGH THE GOLF BALL TO A 3/4 ACCELERATED FINISH. DO NOT ATTEMPT TO ASSIST THE BALL IN THE AIR AS THAT WILL ONLY LEAD TO DISASTER. YOUR PLAYING BUDDIES MAY NOT BE TOO HAPPY WITH YOUR ATTEMPTING TO REMOVE THEIR HEADS FROM THEIR BODIES.

LET THE CLUBS DO THE WORK THEY ARE DESIGNED TO DO.

AGAIN AS IN ALL GOLF SHOTS LET THE COMPUTER DETERMINE THE POWER REQUIRED.

CHAPTER 12

KNOCK DOWN SHOT

<u>KNOCK DOWN SHOT</u>

THE KNOCK DOWN SHOT IS SIMPLY A VARIATION OF THE PITCH SHOT.

WHEN DONE PROPERLY THE GOLF BALL WILL FLY MUCH LOWER THAN NORMAL WHILE MAINTAINING THE BACK SPIN REQUIRED TO HAVE IT STOP QUICKLY WHEN IT LANDS ON THE GREEN.

PLAY THE BALL BACK IN YOUR STANCE, HANDS FORWARD AND APPROXIMATELY 60% OF YOUR WEIGHT FORWARD. NOW IT IS THE SAME SWING AS THE PITCH SHOT. I.E.

3/4 BACK, HIT DOWN HARD AND FOLLOW THROUGH 3/4 WAY ONLY. THE BALL WILL FEEL LIKE IT HAS JUMPED OFF THE FACE OF YOUR CLUB AND WILL MAINTAIN A LOT OF BACK SPIN.

YOU CAN USE A MUCH LOWER LOFTED CLUB WITH THIS SHOT THAN YOU CAN WITH THE PITCH SHOT. EXPERIMENT WITH DIFFERENT CLUBS TO FIND OUT HOW EACH WILL REACT.

ANOTHER NAME FOR THIS SHOT IS THE PUNCH SHOT. IF YOU WATCH TIGER WOODS HE USES A VARIATION OF THIS SHOT OFF THE TEE WITH A THREE WOOD AND/OR 2 IRON.

LET YOUR COMPUTER JUDGE THE POWER REQUIRED FOR THIS SHOT.

CHAPTER 13

SAND PLAY

SAND PLAY

I CHUCKLE WHEN I THINK OF THE TYPICAL AMATEURS REACTION TO THE DREADED SAND SHOT. THIS IS ACTUALLY THE EASIEST SHOT IN GOLF AS IT IS THE ONLY ONE WHERE YOU DON'T HAVE TO HIT THE GOLF BALL. IT REALLY IS A SIMPLE SHOT WHEN YOU UNDERSTAND IT.

IF ALL AMATEURS WERE ABLE TO PRACTICE THIS SHOT FOR A COUPLE OF HOURS EACH DAY, I WOULD SUGGEST THAT THEY USE THE PROFESSIONAL METHOD OF OPENING THEIR SAND WEDGE AND

OPENING THEIR STANCE. THERE IS
HOWEVER A MUCH SIMPLER METHOD OF
DOING THE SAND SHOT AND THAT IS TO
STAY SQUARE TO THE TARGET LINE AND
LINE THE CLUB FACE UP AS YOU WOULD
NORMALLY DO.

YOU WILL BE FACED WITH BASICALLY
THREE DIFFERENT TYPES OF LIES IN A
SAND BUNKER...A GOOD LIE WHERE THE
BALL IS SITTING UP ON TOP OF THE
SAND....A FRIED EGG WHERE THE BALL IS
BELOW THE TOP OF THE SAND....AND THE
EVIL BURIED LIE WHERE THE BALL IS
ACTUALLY PLUGGED DEEPLY INTO THE
SAND.

ALL OF THESE SHOTS HAVE BASICALLY THE SAME TYPE OF A SWING. IT IS A

"U"

SHAPED SWING. YOU WANT TO FEEL LIKE YOU ARE DRAWING A "U" WITH YOUR HANDS WHEN YOU DO THIS SWING. A GOOD WAY TO PRACTICE THIS SWING IS TO DRAW A STRAIGHT LINE IN THE SAND AND MAKE A BUNCH OF SWINGS MAKING SURE YOUR CLUB HITS THE LINE IN THE MIDDLE AND THAT WHAT EVER SAND YOU HIT YOU THROW OUT OF THE BUNKER.. THE "U" SHAPED SWING NEEDS NO MORE POWER THAN A NORMAL GOLF SWING FROM THE SAME DISTANCE. THE "U" SHAPED SWING IS A 3/4 SWING BACK AND AN ACCELERATED 3/4 SWING FORWARD. MAKE SURE YOUR

SWING DOESN'T STOP ONCE YOU MAKE CONTACT WITH THE SAND. IT IS CRITICAL THAT IT IS ACCELERATED TO A FINISH.

ON A GOOD LIE, PLAY THE BALL SLIGHTLY FORWARD OF THE CENTER OF YOUR STANCE. ON A BAD LIE (FRIED EGG OR BURIED) PLAY THE BALL BEHIND THE CENTER OF YOUR STANCE.

WHEN YOU PRACTICE THIS SHOT, DRAW A CIRCLE AROUND THE GOLF BALL IN THE BUNKER. NOW ALL YOU HAVE TO DO IS DO THE 3/4 "U" SHAPED SWING AND MAKE SURE THAT ALL THE SAND IN THE CIRCLE IS THROWN OUT OF THE BUNKER. IF YOU CONCENTRATE ON THE CIRCLE AND

THROWING THE SAND IN IT OUT OF THE BUNKER...THE BALL WILL GO WITH IT. DO NOT ATTEMPT TO ASSIST THE GOLF CLUB OR LIFT THE BALL. THE SAND IRON IS A SPECIALITY CLUB THAT HAS A VERY WIDE SOLE AND IT WILL TAKE CARE OF ITSELF IF YOU LET IT DO ITS JOB. YOUR ASSISTANCE TO HELPING THE CLUB LIFT THE BALL WILL NOT BE APPRECIATED BY THE SAND WEDGE AND IT WILL USUALLY SHOW YOU ITS DISPLEASURE WITH YOUR UNWANTED ASSISTANCE BY LETTING YOU EITHER RE-HIT THE SHOT FROM A FEW FEET CLOSER TO THE HOLE OR GIVE YOU THE PLEASURE OF GOING 30 - 50 YARDS ON THE OTHER SIDE OF THE GREEN AND TRYING TO FIND THE BALL.

IF YOU DRAW A CIRCLE AROUND THE BALL DURING PRACTICE YOUR COMPUTER WILL ACTUALLY SHOW YOU THAT CIRCLE WHEN YOU ARE IN A BUNKER DURING A ROUND OF GOLF....AH, THE OLD COMPUTER...WHAT AN AMAZING THING IT TRULY IS...

IF YOU HAVE A BALL BURIED UNDER THE LIP OF A BUNKER, PLAY IT AS YOU WOULD NORMALLY PLAY A BAD LIE (BACK OF CENTER) AND MAKE YOUR SWING IN THIS MANNER. PICK THE CLUB UP AT A VERY STEEP ANGLE (AND I DO MEAN STEEP) AND SLAM IT DOWN HARD ON TOP OF THE GOLF BALL. THE FORCE OF YOUR HIT AND THE

LOFT OF THE SAND WEDGE WILL CAUSE THE BALL TO ROLL UP ITS FACE AND POP DIRECTLY UP INTO THE AIR, WHEN IT HITS THE GREEN IT WILL HAVE A LOT OF TOP SPIN ON IT AND IT WILL JUMP TOWARDS THE HOLE. NOTE: DO NOT ATTEMPT TO FOLLOW THROUGH WITH THIS SHOT AS YOU COULD HURT YOURSELF, SIMPLY SLAM THE CLUB INTO THE SAND.

A GOOD LIE WILL EXIT THE BUNKER IN A HIGH AND SOFT MANNER. A BAD LIE WILL COME OUT MUCH LOWER AND HOTTER. THE WORSE THE LIE THE LOWER AND HOTTER IT WILL COME OUT.

IF YOU HAVE A LONG BUNKER SHOT OR A FAIRWAY BUNKER SHOT, SIMPLY PLAY THE BALL BACK IN YOUR STANCE AS IT IS CRITICAL THAT YOU CONTACT THE BALL BEFORE THE SAND. TAKE A CLUB WITH ENOUGH LOFT TO CLEAR THE LIP OF THE BUNKER THAT IS IN FRONT OF YOU.

THE OBJECT OF THE SAND SHOT FOR MOST AMATEURS IS TO GET THE BALL OUT OF THE BUNKER. USE A LITTLE COMMON SENSE AND THIS METHOD OF SAND PLAY AND IT WILL BE EASY. AGAIN AS IN ALL SHOTS, LET THE COMPUTER DETERMINE THE POWER REQUIRED.

BY THE WAY, THERE ARE NO SAND TRAPS, THEY ARE BUNKERS...CALL THEM AS SUCH AND A LOT OF THE NEGATIVE THOUGHTS WILL DISAPPEAR.

CHAPTER 14

TROUBLE SHOTS

TROUBLE SHOTS

DOWNHILL LIES: WHEN YOU HAVE A DOWN HILL LIE IT IS IMPORTANT THAT YOU ALIGN YOUR SHOULDERS TO THAT OF THE SLOPE. IF YOU DO NOT YOU WILL HAVE A TENDENCY TO HIT BEHIND THE GOLF BALL. USUALLY YOU WILL WANT TO TAKE ONE LESS CLUB THAN NORMAL AS THE BALL WILL LEAVE THE CLUB FACE A LOT LOWER AND HOTTER THAN YOU EXPECT IT TO. YOU WILL ALSO WANT TO PLAY THE BALL A LITTLE FURTHER BACK IN YOUR STANCE TO PROMOTE STRIKING THE GOLF BALL FIRST.

UPHILL LIES: AGAIN YOU MUST ALIGN YOUR SHOULDERS TO THAT OF THE SLOPE. TAKE ONE EXTRA CLUB THAN YOU WOULD NORMALLY HIT AS THE UP SLOPE WILL TEND TO ADD LOFT TO THE CLUB YOU ARE USING. THE BALL WILL COME OFF THE CLUB FACE WITH A HIGHER TRAJECTORY AND LAND SOFTER THAN YOU EXPECT.

SIDE HILL - BALL ABOVE FEET: YOU WILL NEED TO CHOKE DOWN ON YOUR CLUB AS THE BALL IS CLOSER TO YOU THAN IT NORMALLY IS. AIM A LITTLE RIGHT OF YOUR INTENDED TARGET AS THE BALL WILL NORMALLY FLY A LITTLE FURTHER LEFT THAN USUAL.

SIDE HILL - BALL BELOW FEET: YOU WILL NEED TO PROMOTE A GREATER KNEE FLEX THAN NORMAL AS THE BALL IS FURTHER AWAY FROM YOU THAN IT USUALLY IS. AIM A LITTLE TO THE LEFT OF YOUR INTENDED TARGET AS THE BALL WILL NORMALLY TRAVEL FURTHER TO THE RIGHT THAN ITS USUAL FLIGHT.

BALL IN THICK ROUGH: THIS CAN BE A VERY DANGEROUS GOLF SHOT AS THE LONG GRASS WILL TEND TO WRAP AROUND THE SHAFT AND CLOSE THE CLUB FACE AT IMPACT. THIS WILL CAUSE THE BALL TO TAKE A QUICK DIP TO THE LEFT AND CAN LEAD TO LOTS OF PROBLEMS. COMMON SENSE SHOULD TELL YOU THAT YOU ARE

NOT NORMALLY GOING TO ADVANCE THIS TYPE OF LIE VERY FAR. YOUR OBJECTIVE IS TO GET THE BALL BACK INTO PLAY. YOU MAY WANT TO USE A LOFTED WEDGE FOR THIS SHOT AS IT WILL CUT THROUGH THE GRASS EASIER THAN A LOWER LOFTED CLUB. SOME OF THE UTILITY WOODS ARE MADE TO GO THROUGH GRASS WITH LESS OF A CHANCE OF BEING GRABBED BY THE GRASS. DISCUSS THIS WITH YOUR PRO AND HE/SHE CAN MOST LIKELY STEER YOU IN THE RIGHT DIRECTION. REMEMBER, ERR ON THE SIDE OF CAUTION AND YOU JUST MIGHT BE PUTTING FOR A PAR OR BOGIE INSTEAD OF A TRIPLE OR WORSE.

INTO THE WIND: REFER TO THE KNOCK DOWN SECTION IN THIS BOOK AND TAKE EXTRA CLUB TO COMPENSATE FOR THE LESSER DISTANCE THAT THE WIND AGAINST THE BALL WILL CAUSE.

TRANSITION AREA: REFER AGAIN TO THE KNOCK DOWN SHOT OR EVEN THE LONG BUNKER SHOT. YOU ARE ALLOWED TO GROUND YOUR CLUB IN A TRANSITION AREA.

THERE WILL BE TIMES WHEN YOU HAVE NO SHOT AND WILL HAVE TO TAKE RELIEF IN ACCORDANCE TO THE RULES OF GOLF. TAKE YOUR PUNISHMENT AND YOU WILL NORMALLY SHOOT A LOWER SCORE ON

THAT HOLE THAN IF YOU TRIED AN IMPOSSIBLE RECOVERY SHOT.

THERE IS AN "IF" RULE ON HOW TO SCORE IN GOLF. WHEN YOU HAVE A SHOT THAT YOU ARE ATTEMPTING AND THE WORD "IF" ENTERS YOUR THOUGHTS.....DON'T HIT THIS SHOT....9 TIMES OUT OF 10 IT WILL FAIL AND YOUR SCORE WILL BE HIGH. AN EXAMPLE OF AN "IF" SHOT IS WHEN YOU SAY TO YOURSELF SOMETHING LIKE THIS ....I CAN MAKE THIS SHOT "IF" I MISS THAT TREE, "IF" I THEN CLEAR THE HAZZARD AND "IF" I AVOID THE BUNKER.

REMEMBER GOD HATES A COWARD....BUT HE'S NOT TOO FOND OF A FOOL EITHER..

CHAPTER 15

HITTING WOODS VERSUS IRONS

HITTING WOODS VERSUS IRONS

ALTHOUGH THE SWING WITH A WOOD AND AN IRON ARE VERY SIMILAR THEY ARE ALSO VERY DIFFERENT.

AN IRON IS SWUNG IN A STEEP DESCENDING MANNER WHERE AS A WOOD IS SWUNG IN A MORE SWEEPING MOTION.

WHEN YOU TAKE YOUR STANCE WITH AN IRON, REMEMBER THE BUTT OF IT IS ONE FIST FROM YOUR GROIN. THE SWING GOES BACK AND UP ON A FAIRLY STEEP ANGLE . BY KEEPING YOUR LEFT ARM

COMFORTABLY STRAIGHT IT WILL ASSIST YOU IN NOT GOING UP TOO STEEP AND HAVING THE CLUB TOO CLOSE TO YOUR BODY WHEN IT IS IN THE TRAY POSITION. ONCE YOU HAVE REACHED THE BACK SWINGS MAXIMUM POSITION YOU THEN THROW EVERY THING FORWARD BY COMING DOWN ON THE GOLF BALL AND FINISHING HIGH AND PRETTY.

WHEN YOU TAKE YOUR STANCE WITH A WOODEN CLUB THE BUTT OF IT IS TWO FISTS FROM YOUR GROIN AS IT IS A MUCH WIDER AND LONGER SWING THAN THAT OF AN IRON. EXTEND THE WOOD BACK AWAY FROM THE BALL BY KEEPING THE HEAD OF THE WOOD AS LOW TO THE GROUND AS

YOU CAN, THIS WILL PROMOTE A WIDE TAKE AWAY. ONCE THE CLUB HAS REACHED YOUR MAXIMUM EXTENSION GOING BACK SIMPLY TAKE IT UP TO THE TRAY POSITION. WHEN YOU THROW THE WOOD FORWARD YOU WANT TO FEEL AS IF YOU ARE ACTUALLY SWEEPING THE BALL OFF THE TOP OF THE TEE OR GRASS. YOU NEVER WANT TO HIT DOWN ON A WOOD UNLESS YOU HAVE A PERSONAL RELATIONSHIP WITH THE GOLF GODS. FINISH YOUR SWING HIGH AND PRETTY.

TO PRACTICE THE DIFFERENCE BETWEEN A WOOD SWING AND AN IRON SWING HERE IS AN EASY WAY OF DOING SO. WHEN YOU ARE ON THE PRACTICE RANGE

PUT A TEE IN THE GROUND AND LEAVE APPROXIMATELY 1 INCH ABOVE THE GRASS. WITH AN IRON PRACTICE SWINGING AND BREAKING THE TEE OFF JUST BELOW THE SURFACE OF THE GROUND. WITH A WOOD PRACTICE BARELY CLIPPING THE TOP OF THE TEE SO THAT IT COMES OUT OF THE GROUND IN ONE PIECE. IF YOUR PRACTICE RANGE HAS RUBBER MATS THIS EXERCISE CAN BE DONE BY HITTING THE BOTTOM OF THE MATS RUBBER TEE WITH YOUR IRONS AND BARELY CLIPPING THE TOP OF IT WITH YOUR WOODS SWING.

PRACTICE THE DIFFERENCE BETWEEN THESE DIFFERENT CLUBS AND YOU WILL

Cec McFarlane

LEARN TO HIT BOTH A LOT BETTER THAN
YOU HAVE BEEN DOING.

CHAPTER 16

THE 60% WEDGE

THE 60% WEDGE

THE 60% WEDGE IS ONE OF THE GREATEST TOOLS THAT YOU CAN CARRY IN YOUR BAG, BUT YOU HAD BETTER LEARN HOW TO HIT IT.

MOST AMATEURS WILL SKULL THE 60% WEDGE OR DRIBBLE THE BALL IN A VERY UNSIGHTLY MANNER AS THEY HAVE NOT TAKEN THE TIME TO LEARN THAT THIS CLUB REQUIRES AN UNIQUE GOLF SWING TO BE SUCCESSFUL USING IT.

THE 60% WEDGE IS NEVER HIT WITH MORE THAN A 3/4 SWING. THIS WEDGE IS TAKEN UP VERY STEEP IN THE BACK SWING AND THE DOWN SWING IS VERY VICIOUS AS YOU WANT TO HIT DOWN ON THE BALL WITH FORCE. A THOUGHT THAT YOU COULD HAVE IN MIND IS TO THINK OF SPANKING THE BALL HARD OR SAYING "BAD BALL" WHEN YOU DESCEND UPON THE BALL.

THE HARDER YOU HIT THE 60% WEDGE THE HIGHER AND SOFTER IT WILL GO. THIS HARD SWING TAKES A LOT OF PRACTICE AND CONFIDENCE WHEN YOU TRY IT. MOST AMATEURS ARE AFRAID TO HIT AS HARD AS IS REQUIRED FOR MOST OF THEIR WEDGE SHOTS; ESPECIALLY THE 60% OR LOFT

WEDGE. THEY HAVE A TENDENCY TO TRY AND HELP THE BALL IN THE AIR OR TO SCOOP THEIR WEDGES. THE NEXT TIME YOU ATTEMPT A WEDGE SHOT TRY TO KEEP THE BALL FROM GETTING INTO THE AIR AND YOU WILL BE SURPRISED AT HOW HIGH IT WILL GO. REMEMBER GOLF IS A GAME OF OPPOSITES, YOU WANT THE BALL TO GO LOW; TRY TO MAKE IT GO HIGH....YOU WANT THE BALL TO GO HIGH TRY TO MAKE IT GO LOW.

THE HARDER YOU HIT A 60% WEDGE THE HIGHER IT WILL GO DUE TO THE EXTREME AMOUNT OF LOFT ON THE CLUB.

ONCE YOU LEARN TO HIT A 60% WEDGE PROPERLY YOU WILL FIND THAT YOU CAN REALLY CONTROL IT'S HEIGHT AND DISTANCE BY PLAYING IT FURTHER FORWARD FOR MORE HEIGHT AND FURTHER BACK FOR LESS HEIGHT. REMEMBER THAT A 60% WEDGE IS A SPECIALITY SHOT, THUS ALWAYS MAKE SURE YOUR WEIGHT IS FORWARD AND THAT YOUR HANDS STAY IN FRONT OF THE GOLF BALL. DO NOT BE AFRAID TO HIT THE DARN THING, IT WILL OBEY ONCE IT UNDERSTANDS WHO IT'S MASTER IS.

WITH PRACTICE YOU WILL FIND THE 60% WEDGE A REAL FRIEND AND NOT JUST A CLUB THAT IS IN YOUR BAG TO IMPRESS

YOUR PLAYING PARTNERS AND SIMPLY ADDS WEIGHT TO YOUR ALREADY OVER STUFFED GOLF BAG.

CHAPTER 17

READING BERMUDA

GREENS

READING BERMUDA GREENS

MOST GOLFERS HAVE A DIFFICULT TIME READING BERMUDA GREENS AND YET WHEN YOU KNOW WHAT TO LOOK FOR THEY ARE REALLY RATHER SIMPLE.

BERMUDA GRASS TENDS TO GROW TOWARD THE HOTTEST SUN POSITION AND THAT IS NORMALLY THE SOUTH WEST, THUS IN MOST CASES THE GRAIN WILL RUN IN THAT DIRECTION REGARDLESS OF THE SLOPE OF THE GREEN, WATER RUN OFF OR THE CONTOUR OF THE LAND AROUND THE GREEN. THIS IS QUITE DIFFERENT THAN THE

NORTHERN GRASSES BUT ONCE YOU UNDERSTAND IT YOU HAVE A BETTER CHANCE AT SUCCESSFULLY PUTTING BERMUDA GREENS.

IF YOU DO NOT KNOW WHERE SOUTH WEST IS, THERE ARE TWO SIMPLE METHODS OF READING BERMUDA GRASS. THE FIRST ONE IS TO LOOK AT THE CUP CUT INTO THE GREEN, YOU WILL NOTICE A SMOOTH EDGE AND A RAGGED LOOKING EDGE. WHEN A GREENS KEEPER CUTS THE HOLE HIS EQUIPMENT CUTS THE GRASS VERY CLEANLY. THE BERMUDA THAT IS STILL ATTACHED TO THE GROUND WILL BE SMOOTH AS IT STILL IS ATTACHED TO ITS ROOTS. THE TIP OF THE BERMUDA OR THE

GROWING EDGE WILL BE CUT OFF LEAVING NO SUPPORT FOR THESE STRANDS OF BERMUDA, THUS IT WILL HAVE A RAGGED LOOK TO IT. THEREFORE THE GRASS IS GROWING FROM THE SMOOTH SIDE TO THE RAGGED SIDE OR IN OTHER WORDS THAT IS THE DIRECTION OF THE GRAIN. THE SECOND METHOD IS TO LOOK INTO THE GRASS FROM A DISTANCE. IF THE GRASS LOOKS DARK THE GRAIN IS COMING TOWARDS YOU, IF IT LOOKS SHINY THE GRAIN IS GOING AWAY FROM YOU.

WHEN YOU PUTT BERMUDA GREENS YOU MUST BE AWARE THAT AS THE BALL TENDS TO SLOW DOWN OR LOSE ITS FORWARD MOMENTUM THE GRAIN WILL REALLY

EFFECT WHAT HAPPENS TO THE BALL. BERMUDA GROWS BASICALLY IN AN UPRIGHT MANNER WITH A SLIGHT LEAN TOWARDS THE HOTTEST SUN POSITION. IT WILL DRASTICALLY TURN A GOLF BALL PUTTING ACROSS THESE SLIGHTLY BENT GRASS BLADES. IF YOU ARE PUTTING WITH THE GRAIN IT WILL HAVE VERY LITTLE EFFECT ON THE GOLF BALL AS IT SLOWS DOWN, HOWEVER IT WILL BE 2-3 TIMES FASTER THAN PUTTING INTO THE GRAIN., EVEN IF YOU ARE PUTTING UPHILL. KNOWING THE DIRECTION OF THE GRAIN IS ABSOLUTELY CRITICAL WHEN YOU PUTT ON BERMUDA. AS AN EXAMPLE: IF YOU HAVE A SIDE HILL PUTT ON BERMUDA GRASS AND THE BALL WILL BE GOING INTO THE GRAIN,

THIS GRAIN WILL TEND TO REDUCE THE BREAKING OF THE GOLF BALL AS IT SLOWS DOWN. THIS FOOLS A LOT OF PLAYERS AS IF THEY HAD A STEEP SIDE HILL PUTT IN THE NORTH, ITS "KATIE BAR THE DOOR, THIS IS GOING TO BE QUICK" THE SAME PUTT ON BERMUDA WITH THE GRAIN GOING UP THE SLOPE WILL BREAK LESS THAN A THIRD OF THE NORTHERN PUTT AS THE BERMUDA FINGERS (GRAIN) WILL STOP THE BALL FROM MOVING AS MUCH AS YOU FEEL IT SHOULD. IF YOU WERE PUTTING ON A SIDE HILL WITH THE GRAIN GOING DOWN THE HILL, THE BALL WILL BREAK AS IF IT HIT SOMETHING THAT THREW IT COMPLETELY SIDEWAYS AS IT SLOWS DOWN, IT WILL

THEN PICK UP LOTS OF SPEED AS THERE IS NO GRAIN TO HELP STOP IT.

YOU CAN ACTUALLY HAVE SEVERE DOWNHILL PUTTS GOING INTO THE BERMUDA GRAIN THAT WILL BE SO SLOW YOU MAY WANT TO USE YOUR DRIVER AND A FULL SWING.

PRACTICE READING BERMUDA GRASS AND PRACTICE VARIOUS ANGLES WITH YOUR PUTTS TO SEE THE EFFECT THIS GRASS HAS ON THE GOLF BALL.

LEARN TO READ BERMUDA AND IT IS FUN TO PUTT.....THEN AGAIN SOME PEOPLE LIKE ROOT CANALS.

CHAPTER 18

HOW TO PRACTICE

HOW TO PRACTICE

MOST AMATEURS DO NOT IMPROVE THEIR GOLF GAME AS THEY HAVE NO CONCEPT OF PROPER PRACTICE METHODS.

TIME AFTER TIME I SEE AMATEURS GO TO A DRIVING RANGE AND BASICALLY HIT THEIR WOODS AND THE OCCASIONAL IRON. THIS IS TOTALLY COUNTER PRODUCTIVE TO THEIR ABILITY TO PLAY SOLID GOLF AND TO SCORE WELL.

LOOK AT THE STATISTICS BELOW TO SEE WHAT I MEAN.

TAKE AN AVERAGE 18 HOLE PAR 72 REGULATION GOLF COURSE. THERE ARE NORMALLY 4 PAR 3 HOLES, 4 PAR 5 HOLES AND 10 PAR 4 HOLES. THAT MEANS THAT A SCRATCH GOLFER WOULD NORMALLY REQUIRE THE FOLLOWING USE OF CLUBS IF HE WERE TO SHOOT AN EVEN PAR ROUND OF 72.

14 DRIVERS OR 19.4% OF HIS STROKES

4 FAIRWAY WOODS OR 5.6% OF HIS STROKES

8 MIDDLE IRONS OR 11.1% OF HIS STROKES

10 SHORT IRONS OR 13.9% OF HIS STROKES

36 PUTTS OR 50.0% OF HIS STROKES

WHAT THIS MEANS IS THAT TO SHOOT PAR GOLF(AND WE KNOW MOST GOLFERS WILL NEVER COME CLOSE TO PAR, THUS THEY WILL USE A LARGER PERCENTAGE OF SHOTS FROM 100 YARDS IN AND ON THE GREEN,) YOU WILL HAVE USED 63.9% OF YOUR SHOTS FROM WITHIN 100 YARDS OF THE GREEN AND LESS THAN 20% WILL BE WITH THE THUNDER STICK OR DRIVER.

IF THIS DOESN'T START YOU THINKING ABOUT HOW YOU PRACTICE AND HOW YOUR CURRENT PRACTICE HABITS ARE WRONG YOU MAY WANT TO CONSIDER TAKING UP TENNIS AS GOLF WILL NEVER BE ANYTHING BUT A FRUSTRATION TO YOU.

IF YOU WANT TO BE SERIOUS ABOUT PRACTICING AND IMPROVING YOUR GAME HERE IS A PRACTICE ROUTINE THAT YOU COULD FOLLOW. WHEN YOU ARRIVE AT THE PRACTICE RANGE SPEND A FEW MINUTES GETTING LOOSE. IT WILL MAKE YOUR PRACTICE SESSION EASIER AND REDUCE YOUR ODDS OF AN INJURY.

NOW, SPEND AT LEAST 10 MINUTES ON THE PUTTING GREEN, THEN 10 MINUTES HITTING SHORT CHIPS, THEN 10 MINUTES HITTING LONG CHIPS, THEN 10 MINUTES HITTING SHORT PITCH SHOTS, THEN 10 MINUTES HITTING LONG PITCH SHOTS AND THEN 10 MINUTES IN THE SAND BUNKER.

NOW YOU ARE READY TO GO TO THE HITTING AREA AND SAY GET A BUCKET OF 60 GOLF BALLS. (IT IS NOT THE QUANTITY OF BALLS THAT YOU HIT IT IS THE QUALITY). START WITH YOUR SAND WEDGE AND HIT 4 BALLS WITH EACH AND EVERY IRON, THEN HIT 5 BALLS WITH BOTH YOUR 3 AND 5 WOODS. YOU WILL NOW HAVE 14 BALLS LEFT TO HIT WITH YOUR DRIVER. AFTER YOU HAVE HIT ALL OF YOUR PRACTICE BALLS, FINISH YOUR PRACTICE SESSION BY SPENDING ANOTHER 10 MINUTES ON THE PUTTING GREEN. IT WILL NOT ONLY COOL YOU DOWN IT WILL BE PRODUCTIVE TO YOUR SPENDING TIME WHERE IT WILL HELP YOU THE MOST.

IF YOU HAVE THE WILL POWER TO FOLLOW THIS PRACTICE ROUTINE, YOU WILL TAKE AT LEAST 5 STROKES OFF YOUR GAME WITHIN A MONTH.

WHEN YOU ARRIVE AT A GOLF COURSE TO PLAY, GET THERE WITH ENOUGH TIME TO HIT A FEW IRONS AND WOODS ON THE RANGE TO GET YOUR RHYTHM AND FEEL THAT YOU HAVE GOOD TEMPO. FINISH YOUR PRE ROUND WARM UP ON THE PRACTICE GREEN.

WHEN YOU WARM UP PRIOR TO PLAYING, IT IS NOT A PRACTICE SESSION IT IS SIMPLY GETTING YOURSELF READY TO INCORPORATE ALL THE HARD WORK YOU

HAVE DONE TO PREPARE YOURSELF TO PLAY GOLF. ONCE YOU HAVE HIT ENOUGH BALLS IN YOUR PRE GAME WARM UP TO FEEL LOOSE, THAT IS ALL YOU NEED TO DO. WHAT YOU HAVE BROUGHT TO THE GOLF COURSE IS WHAT YOU HAVE TO LIVE WITH ON ANY GIVEN DAY. YOU ARE NOT ABOUT TO SUDDENLY FIND A GOLF SWING ONCE YOU HAVE STARTED TO PLAY. LACK OF BEING PREPARED PROPERLY BY A LACK OF GOOD PRACTICE METHODS WILL TAKE THEIR TOLL.

BECOME A BETTER PLAYER BY LEARNING HOW TO PRACTICE...

CHAPTER 19

LESSONS

LESSONS

LESSONS ARE A NEEDED REQUIREMENT TO LEARN GOLF. MANY AMATEURS PROUDLY ANNOUNCE THAT THEY HAVE NEVER TAKEN A PROFESSIONAL LESSON IN THEIR LIVES. USUALLY THEY DIDN'T REALLY HAVE TO ANNOUNCE IT

YOU CANNOT SEE YOURSELF OR WHAT YOU ARE DOING AND THAT IN ITSELF MAKES SELF LEARNING NEXT TO IMPOSSIBLE.

IF YOU TAKE A GOLF LESSON OR SERIES OF LESSONS THERE ARE A FEW THINGS THAT YOU NEED TO KNOW.

MODERN TEACHERS USE VIDEO TAPE AS WHEN YOU CAN SEE WHAT YOU ARE DOING IT MAKES IT A LOT EASIER FOR YOU TO IMPROVE. MAKE SURE THE VIDEO TAPE IS YOURS AT THE END OF THE LESSON. VIDEO ALSO ASSISTS THE TEACHER IN SEEING EXACTLY WHAT IS HAPPENING TO CAUSE A PROBLEM. IT IS VIRTUALLY IMPOSSIBLE FOR ANYONE TO SEE WHAT IS GOING ON IN A PERSONS GOLF SWING AS IT HAPPENS TOO QUICKLY FOR THE HUMAN EYE TO PICK EVERYTHING UP. IF YOUR TEACHER DOES

NOT USE VIDEO THEY MUST BE ONE HECK OF A GOOD GUESSER.

TRY AND AVOID THE 3 - 5 DAY GOLF PACKAGES AND LARGE GROUPS BECAUSE THEY WILL GIVE YOU INFORMATION OVER LOAD AND WILL LIMIT THE ACTUAL AMOUNT OF INFORMATION THAT YOU WILL BE ABLE TO RETAIN. YOU ALSO WILL BE PAYING A VERY HIGH RATE FOR NON PERSONAL ATTENTION.

BEFORE YOU COMMIT TO A PACKAGE OF LESSONS FROM ANY PRO TAKE A HALF HOUR LESSON FROM HIM/HER TO SEE HOW THE TWO OF YOU RELATE AND IF THE PROS STYLE IS ONE TO WHICH YOU FEEL YOU

CAN LEARN FROM. NOT ALL PROS ARE GOOD TEACHERS NOR CAN ALL PROS RELATE TO EVERYONE. FIND THIS INFORMATION OUT BEFORE YOU COMMIT TO AN EXPENSIVE SERIES OF LESSONS.

IF A PRO STARTS THROWING BIG WORDS AT YOU, SUCH AS PRONATE, IN AN ATTEMPT TO IMPRESS YOU, THAT PRO MOST LIKELY HAS LITTLE KNOWLEDGE OF THE GOLF SWING OR GOLF GAME. RUN TO THE NEAREST EXIT. THERE ARE A LOT OF 50 & 75 CENT WORDS IN GOLF THAT YOU REALLY DON'T NEED TO KNOW ABOUT.

DO NOT EXPECT THAT A SINGLE LESSON OR A FEW LESSONS WILL IMMEDIATELY

CORRECT YOUR PROBLEMS. MOST OF YOUR PROBLEMS HAVE TAKEN YOU YEARS TO REFINE AND YOU WILL HAVE TO WORK VERY HARD TO GET THEM OUT OF YOUR SYSTEM. YOUR PROBLEM HAS BECOME A HABIT AND THUS WILL TAKE A LOT OF EFFORT FROM YOU TO CORRECT.

A TEACHING PROS JOB IS TO DEFINE THE "CAUSE" OF YOUR PROBLEMS AND SHOW YOU WHAT YOU MUST DO TO CORRECT THEM. THERE IS NO PRO THAT CAN CORRECT THEM FOR YOU.. BE VERY WARY OF A PRO THAT DEFINES YOUR PROBLEM AND FAILS TO SHOW YOU WHAT IS CAUSING THE PROBLEM AND THE SOLUTION TO FIX IT.

IF YOU DO NOT UNDERSTAND SOMETHING THAT THE PRO HAS SAID TO YOU, IT IS YOUR RESPONSIBILITY TO MAKE SURE THAT YOU REALLY DO UNDERSTAND WHAT THE PRO IS TRYING TO GET ACROSS TO YOU. ANY GOOD PRO WILL TAKE THE TIME TO EXPLAIN THINGS IN DETAIL SO THAT YOUR QUESTIONS ARE ANSWERED. REMEMBER THERE ARE NO DUMB QUESTIONS IN GOLF AS IF YOU DO NOT KNOW THE ANSWER THE QUESTION IS NOT DUMB.

IF POSSIBLE WATCH YOUR PRO GIVE A LESSON (DO THIS AT A DISTANCE AS SOME PROS DON'T LIKE TO BE WATCHED...THE BETTER ONES WILL HAVE NO PROBLEM

WITH YOUR INVESTIGATING THEM AND THEIR TEACHING STYLE BEFORE YOU MAKE A DECISION ABOUT TAKING LESSONS FROM THEM). IF POSSIBLE ASK SOME OF THE PRO'S STUDENTS ABOUT THEIR LESSONS AND THE RESULTS THEY FEEL THEY HAVE OBTAINED BY WORKING WITH THIS PARTICULAR PRO.

MOST AMATEURS WATCH TOO MUCH GOLF INSTRUCTION ON T.V., READ TOO MANY BOOKS (THIS ONE OF COURSE IS THE EXCEPTION), AND LISTEN TO TOO MANY PEOPLE ABOUT GOLF AND THE THEORIES OF THE GAME. A LITTLE INFORMATION CAN BE HARMFUL, A LOT OF BAD INFORMATION CAN BE DOWN RIGHT DETRIMENTAL TO

YOUR GOLFING DREAMS AND EXPECTATIONS.

IF YOU DECIDE ON A PARTICULAR PRO, STAY WITH THAT PRO AND DEVELOP A RELATIONSHIP WITH HIM/HER. THERE MUST BE MUTUAL TRUST BETWEEN A PRO AND A STUDENT IF THE STUDENT IS REALLY GOING TO LEARN ANYTHING FROM THE PRO AND THE PRO LEARN WHAT THE STUDENT REALLY FEELS ABOUT GOLF ETC. A LOT OF TIMES A PRO WILL LEARN MORE ABOUT THEIR STUDENTS PROBLEMS BY GOLFING WITH THEM ON A CASUAL BASIS. I GOLF A LOT WITH MY STUDENTS AS I TRULY FEEL I CAN BETTER ASSIST THEM IN OUR LESSONS. MANY TIMES THE PROBLEM THAT

THE STUDENT HAS IS NOT QUITE THAT WHAT THEY THINK IT IS. AS AN EXAMPLE I ONCE HAD A STUDENT THAT WANTED TO CORRECT THEIR CHIPPING. I ASKED TO SEE THE FORM OF CHIPPING THAT HE USED AND IT WAS ALMOST TEXT BOOK PERFECT. I THEN PLAYED A ROUND WITH THIS STUDENT AND FOUND THAT CHIPPING WASN'T HIS PROBLEM, IT WAS HIS DRIVES. HE COULDN'T HIT THEM FAR ENOUGH TO EVEN HAVE A CHANCE AT REACHING THE GREEN ON HIS SECOND SHOT, SO ALL OF HIS CHIPS WERE FROM TWICE THE DISTANCE THAT THEY SHOULD HAVE BEEN. UPON FURTHER INVESTIGATION, I FOUND THAT HIS DRIVER HAD AN EXTRA STIFF SHAFT THAT JOHN DALY COULDN'T HIT.

ONCE I HAD HIS SHAFT CHANGED TO THE PROPER FLEX HIS WHOLE GAME IMPROVED AND I GAINED A LONG TIME FRIEND AND STUDENT. WE LAUGH ABOUT HIS SELF ANALYSIS NOW.

BE CAREFUL WHO YOU TAKE ADVICE FROM AS THERE IS AN UNWRITTEN RULE IN GOLF.......THE HIGHER ONES HANDICAP IS......THE MORE QUALIFIED THEY ARE TO GIVE YOU ADVICE.....THEY CAN NOT DO IT THEMSELVES BUT THEY SURE CAN TELL YOU HOW TO DO IT. THESE PEOPLE MEAN WELL, JUST BE CAREFUL ABOUT LISTENING TO THEM.

CHAPTER 20

GOLF CLUBS

<u>GOLF CLUBS</u>

MOST AMATEURS DO NOT UNDERSTAND THE IMPORTANCE OF HAVING GOLF CLUBS THAT ARE FITTED TO THEM.

FOR EXAMPLE: IF YOU HAVE A CLUB THAT HAS A SHAFT THAT IS TOO STIFF FOR YOU, YOU WILL NEVER BE ABLE TO MAKE THAT CLUB PERFORM TO ITS FULL POTENTIAL. ON THE OTHER HAND, IF YOU HAVE SHAFTS THAT ARE TOO FLEXIBLE FOR YOUR STRENGTH YOU WILL ALSO HAVE MANY PROBLEMS WITH CONSISTENCY AS THEY WILL OVER FLEX ON YOUR DOWN

SWING AND PRODUCE VARIED RESULTS.
USUALLY NEGATIVE.

ALL PROFESSIONALS HAVE SHAFTS THAT
ARE FITTED TO THEM AS THEY REALIZE THE
IMPORTANCE OF SAME. AMATEURS THE
WORLD OVER CONTINUE TO BUY CLUBS
OFF THE RACK WITH LITTLE OR NO
KNOWLEDGE AS TO WHAT THEY ARE
ACTUALLY GETTING.

NORMALLY AN AMATEUR, WHEN
QUESTIONED ABOUT THEIR CLUBS AND THE
SHAFTS THAT THEY ARE HITTING, WILL
REPLY SOMETHING LIKE THIS. "WHEN I WAS
AT THE WONDER GOLF STORE THEY PUT ME
ON A MACHINE AND TESTED ME FOR SWING

SPEED. THEY THEN FITTED ME WITH THE PROPER CLUBS AND SHAFTS. I AM A REGULAR FLEX AND THAT IS WHAT ALL OF MY CLUBS ARE...LOOK IT SAYS SO ON THE SHAFT"

I HATE TO BURST YOUR BUBBLE BUT IN TRUTH THE SALES CLERK AT THE WONDER GOLF STORE HAS ABOUT AS MUCH KNOWLEDGE ABOUT CLUB FITTING AS THE AVERAGE PERSON HAS ABOUT PERFORMING BRAIN SURGERY. THE SO CALLED SWING SPEED MACHINE IS ONE OF THE BIGGEST GIMMICKS THAT HAS EVER HIT THE GOLF MARKET. A TYPICAL OFF THE RACK SET OF CLUBS WILL HAVE SHAFTS IN THE SET THAT VARY ANYWHERE FROM SENIOR FLEX TO EXTRA STIFF. JUST

REMEMBER THAT GOLF CLUB MANUFACTURERS ARE NOT IN THE BUSINESS OF SELLING FITTED SHAFTS, THEY ARE SIMPLY SELLING A PRODUCT THAT THEIR SLICK ADVERTISING PROMOTION HAS CONVINCED YOU ARE THE CLUBS THAT WILL CORRECT ALL OF YOUR GOLFING PROBLEMS.

"YOU CAN NOT BUY A GOLF SWING OFF A SHELF"

IN ORDER TO BE FITTED CORRECTLY A PROFESSIONAL MUST ACTUALLY WATCH YOU HIT GOLF BALLS WITH A VARIETY OF FLEXED SHAFTS. THE PROS KNOWLEDGE AND EXPERTISE COMES FROM YEARS OF

CLUB FITTING AS THERE ARE MANY FACTORS INVOLVED, FAR BEYOND THE SO CALLED SWING SPEED. YOU CAN ACTUALLY CREATE MORE FALSE SWING SPEED WITH JUST YOUR ARMS THAN YOU CAN WITH A PROPER GOLF SWING. POWER AND DISTANCE COMES FROM A COMBINATION OF THINGS THAT PRODUCE MASS, POWER AND SPEED. IF YOU GET FITTED FOR A SET OF CLUBS AND THEN DECIDE TO TAKE GOLF LESSONS TO LEARN THE PROPER SWING, YOU MOST LIKELY WILL HAVE CLUBS THAT ARE NOW COMPLETELY WRONG FOR YOUR POWER AND SWING. WHEN YOU LEARN THE PROPER SWING YOUR ACTUAL POWER WILL BE INCREASED DRASTICALLY. A BETTER PRO WILL SUGGEST THAT YOU FIX YOUR

SWING BY TAKING A FEW SWING LESSONS PRIOR TO BEING FITTED FOR CLUBS.

"YOU ARE ONLY AS GOOD AS YOUR TOOLS ALLOW YOU TO BE"

THERE ARE LOADS OF GREAT GOLF HEADS AND SHAFTS AVAILABLE ON THE MARKET TODAY. BOTH NAME AND NON-NAME BRANDS. ONLY A SEASONED PROFESSIONAL CAN DETERMINE WHAT IS THE CORRECT EQUIPMENT FOR YOU.

ANOTHER GIMMICK IN CLUB FITTING IS TO MEASURE THE DISTANCE FROM THE FLOOR TO YOUR FINGER TIPS. IN REALITY, IF YOU TAKE 20 MEN OR LADIES AND USING

THE SAME SEX, STAND THEM SIDE BY SIDE, AT LEAST 18-19 OF THEIR FINGER TIPS WILL BE THE SAME DISTANCE FROM THE FLOOR, REGARDLESS OF THEIR INDIVIDUAL HEIGHT. THIS IS SIMPLY NATURE AND HOW WE ARE ALL BUILT VERY SIMILAR. MOST RETAILERS REALIZE THAT WHEN IT COMES TO GOLF....B/S BAFFLES BRAINS OR MAKE IT SOUND SCIENTIFIC AND PEOPLE WILL BUY INTO IT.

I WOULD HAZZARD A GUESS THAT AT LEAST 80% OF ALL THE AMATEURS THAT I TEACH COME TO ME WITH IMPROPERLY FITTED CLUBS.

THE IRONIC THING IS THAT A CUSTOM FITTED SET OF CLUBS USUALLY COSTS A LOT LESS THAN THE OFF THE RACK CLUBS THAT YOU ARE PAYING THE MANUFACTURERS ADVERTISING FOR.

THERE IS A CHOICE BETWEEN GRAPHITE AND STEEL SHAFTS. WHICH IS CORRECT FOR YOU DEPENDS ON A LOT OF FACTORS THAT YOU AND YOUR PRO CAN DETERMINE. FOR EXAMPLE, AS YOU GET OLDER AND THE PAIN OF AGING SETS IN; GRAPHITE SHAFTS ARE SOFTER ON YOUR HANDS AND JOINTS. IF YOU ARE STRONG AND LIKE TO REALLY GIVE THE GOLF BALL A GOOD SMASH, THEN STEEL WILL MOST LIKELY BE THE CHOICE FOR YOU.

IN YEARS PAST THERE WAS A DEFINITE INCONSISTENCY IN GRAPHITE SHAFTS. WITH MODERN TECHNOLOGY AND PRODUCTION METHODS THE TOP SHAFT MAKERS ARE EXTREMELY CONSISTENT AND THERE IS AS GOOD QUALITY IN GRAPHITE SHAFTS AS IN STEEL NOW A DAYS.

HOWEVER, BE CAREFUL WHERE YOU GET YOUR CLUBS SHAFTED OR YOU MAY END UP BEING THE ONE THAT REALLY GETS SHAFTED. THERE ARE A LOT OF CHEAPLY MADE STEEL AND GRAPHITE PRODUCTS IN THE MARKET PLACE . WITH THE HELP OF YOUR TRUSTED PRO HE/SHE WILL SEE THAT YOU GET QUALITY.

IF YOU ARE A NEW GOLFER, DO NOT PURCHASE A NEW SET OF CLUBS AND THEN TRY AND LEARN THE GAME. THE GOLF SWING YOU START WITH WILL NOT EVEN BE CLOSE TO THE ONE THAT YOU WILL HAVE IN A COUPLE OF YEARS. YOU CAN PURCHASE A VERY GOOD AND INEXPENSIVE SET OF USED CLUBS FROM YOUR PRO AND THEY WILL DO JUST FINE UNTIL YOU LEARN THE PROPER GOLF SWING. YOU WOULD BE MUCH WISER TO SPEND YOUR DOLLARS ON LESSONS IN THE BEGINNING INSTEAD OF KEEPING UP WITH THE JONES.

BUYER BEWARE.....USE YOUR PROS KNOWLEDGE....AND DON'T GET STUCK WITH

SOMETHING THAT IS DETRIMENTAL TO YOUR JOURNEY IN BEING A GOOD GOLFER.

CHAPTER 21

COURSE MANAGEMENT

<u>COURSE MANAGEMENT</u>

GOLF COURSE MANAGEMENT IS THE MOST IMPORTANT PART IN LEARNING HOW TO SCORE OR IN OTHER WORDS HOW TO SHOOT LOW SCORES.

PROS TALK ABOUT COURSE MANAGEMENT ALL THE TIME BECAUSE THEY UNDERSTAND THAT IT IS ABSOLUTELY CRITICAL TO THEIR GAME.

MOST AMATEURS ARE MORE CONCERNED WITH JUST HITTING A GOLF BALL THAN THEY ARE IN LEARNING HOW TO

SCORE. YOU HAVE TO BE ABLE TO STRIKE A GOLF BALL HOWEVER YOU MUST LEARN TO SCORE THROUGH THE USE OF COURSE MANAGEMENT, OR IN OTHER WORDS YOUR COMPUTER AND A LITTLE COMMON SENSE.

THE FIRST THING THAT YOU MUST LEARN ABOUT COURSE MANAGEMENT IS TO ALWAYS ALLOW YOURSELF TO MISS THE SHOT THAT YOU HAVE PLANNED. VERY SELDOM ARE YOU GOING TO HIT THE PERFECT GOLF SHOT, SO NEVER TRY A SHOT, THAT IF IT FAILS, IT PUTS YOU IN JAIL.

AN EXAMPLE OF PUTTING YOURSELF IN JAIL IS THAT OF SUCKER PINS ON PAR 3'S. THEY ARE OFTEN HIDDEN BEHIND A

BUNKER OR CLOSE TO WATER OR SOME OTHER HAZZARD. TIME AFTER TIME AMATEURS ATTEMPT TO STICK IT ON THE PIN AND MORE OFTEN THAN NOT THEY MISS THE SHOT AND END UP WITH A 5 OR 6 ON THEIR CARD. MOST PROS WILL REALIZE THE POOR ODDS AND FRUITLESSNESS OF GOING FOR THE FLAG AND WILL SHOOT TO THE MIDDLE OF THE GREEN. THEY WILL BE HAPPY WITH A PAR, YET THEY MAY JUST SINK THE ODD LONG PUTT FOR A BIRDIE. IT IS VERY DIFFICULT TO MAKE PAR WHEN YOU ARE HITTING 3 FROM THE TEE OR DROP AREA ON A PAR 3.

YOU LEARN TO SCORE FROM THE GREEN BACK TO THE TEE NOT FROM THE TEE TO

THE GREEN. IF YOU BECOME A GOOD PUTTER IT WILL MAKE YOUR CHIP OR PITCH SHOTS A LOT EASIER; IF YOUR CHIP AND PITCH SHOTS ARE EASY IT WILL TAKE PRESSURE OFF YOUR APPROACH SHOTS AND IF YOUR APPROACH SHOTS ARE EASIER IT WILL TAKE PRESSURE OFF YOUR DRIVES. THINK ABOUT IT AND REFER BACK TO THE SECTION ON HOW TO PRACTICE AND SEE WHERE THE EMPHASIS HAS BEEN PLACED.

NEVER TRY THE "HAIL MARY" SHOT. YOU MAY PULL IT OFF EVERY ONCE IN A WHILE BUT OVER TIME IT WILL EAT YOUR GOLF GAME ALIVE. IF YOU ARE IN TROUBLE, GET THE BALL BACK IN PLAY AND IF THAT

INVOLVES A PENALTY STROKE.... TOUGH.....

YOU HIT IT THERE. YOU CANNOT SCORE IF

YOU ARE CONSTANTLY TRYING MIRACLE

SHOTS. REMEMBER MIRACLES HAPPEN ON

34TH STREET NOT ON THE GOLF COURSE.

TO LEARN GOOD COURSE MANAGEMENT

PLAY WITH YOUR PRO AND WATCH HOW

HE/SHE PLAYS VARIOUS HOLES AND SHOTS.

YOU MAY EVEN WANT TO SPLURGE FOR A

PLAYING LESSON AND THEN YOU CAN ASK A

THOUSAND QUESTIONS AND MAYBE

BECOME A BETTER PLAYER.

A LOT OF AMATEURS, ESPECIALLY

MACHO MEN, PLAY FROM TEES THAT ARE

TOO LONG FOR THEIR ABILITY. THEY CAN

BARELY REACH THE GREEN ON THEIR SECOND SHOT BUT STILL LUMBER ALONG ON THE MISTAKEN PREMISES THAT GOLF IS A GAME OF LENGTH AND POWER. IF THESE MACHO PEOPLE WERE TO PLAY FROM THE REGULAR MEMBER TEES THEY WOULD FIND THAT THEY WILL HAVE TO BECOME COURSE MANAGERS AS THEY WILL NOW BE ABLE TO EASILY REACH THE TROUBLE AREAS OFF THE TEE AND THEY WILL HAVE TO GET USED TO SHOOTING AT PIN POSITIONS ON THEIR SECOND SHOT; NOT JUST HOPING TO GET ENOUGH CLUB ON THE BALL TO GET IT SOMEWHERE AROUND THE GREEN.

AGAIN IF YOU WANT TO LEARN HOW TO SCORE, LEARN COURSE MANAGEMENT AND

SHOT MAKING. ONCE IN A WHILE HIT THAT 3

WOOD OFF THE TEE FOR POSITION INSTEAD

OF GRUNTING THROUGH A DRIVER AND

HOLDING UP THE REST OF THE COURSE

WHILE YOU HUNT FOR THAT SUPER LONG

DRIVE IN THE BUSHES.

CHAPTER 22

GOLF ETIQUETTE

<u>GOLF ETIQUETTE</u>

FOR YOU RELATIVELY NEW GOLFERS HERE ARE A COUPLE OF POINTS TO ASSIST YOU WHEN YOU PLAY YOUR FIRST ROUNDS OF GOLF.

WHEN YOU ARRIVE ON THE FIRST TEE THERE IS USUALLY A SIMPLE METHOD OF DECIDING WHO TEES OFF FIRST. IT CAN BE A VOLUNTEER OR YOU CAN TOSS A TEE IN THE AIR AND THE PLAYERS TEE OFF IN THE ORDER THAT THE TEE POINTS TO THEM.

ONCE YOU BEGIN PLAY THE ORDER OF WHO'S TURN IT IS TO HIT THE BALL IS SIMPLY THE PLAYER FURTHEST AWAY FROM THE GOLF HOLE. AS YOU APPROACH THE GREEN IT IS STILL THE FURTHEST PLAYER AWAY, REGARDLESS IF THEIR BALL IS ON THE GREEN OR NOT.

WHEN YOU ARE ALL ON THE GREEN THE FURTHEST PLAYER AWAY FROM THE HOLE GETS TO PUTT FIRST. ONCE THAT PERSON HAS STARTED PUTTING THEY MAY, AT THEIR OPTION, CONTINUE UNTIL THEIR BALL IS HOLED OUT.

WHEN ANOTHER PLAYER IS PLAYING THEIR SHOT FROM ANYWHERE ON THE

GOLF COURSE, INCLUDING THE GREEN, DO NOT STAND DIRECTLY BEHIND THEIR LINE OF SIGHT. IT WILL BOTHER THEM AS THEY CAN SEE YOU OR YOUR FEET FROM THE CORNER OF THEIR EYES. ON THE GREEN THIS IS ILLEGAL AND IT WILL CAUSE YOU TO BE PENALIZED AS IT IS GETTING UNFAIR ADVANTAGE BY WATCHING THE LINE OF ANOTHER PLAYERS PUTT AND POSSIBLY ASSISTING YOU IN YOUR PUTT.

WHEN ANOTHER PLAYER IS MAKING A STROKE, DO NOT TALK TO THE OTHER PLAYERS, RATTLE COINS IN YOUR POCKET OR MAKE ANY OTHER NOISES OR MOVEMENTS THAT COULD INTERFERE WITH THAT PLAYERS CONCENTRATION. TO DO SO

IS CONSIDERED TO BE VERY IGNORANT AND IF DONE ENOUGH TIMES TO THE WRONG PLAYER COULD RESULT IN YOUR HAVING TO USE YOUR GOLF TOWEL TO STOP THE BLEEDING FROM YOUR NOSE.

WHEN ANOTHER PLAYER IS PUTTING YOU MAY BE ASKED TO TEND OR HOLD THE FLAG FOR THEM. SIMPLY MAKE SURE YOUR SHADOW DOESN'T COVER THE HOLE AND HOLD THE FLAG AT THE TOP TO AVOID THE WIND FLAPPING IT AND DISTRACTING THE PUTTER. YOU MUST REMOVE THE FLAG AS SOON AS THE PLAYER MAKES THEIR STROKE AS IF THEIR BALL COMES INTO CONTACT WITH THE FLAG STICK OR FLAG THEY WILL BE PENALIZED TWO

STROKES..OOPS TIME TO USE THAT GOLF TOWEL TO AGAIN STOP THE BLEEDING OF YOUR NOSE. DO NOT LAY THE FLAG DOWN AS SOON AS YOU REMOVE IT AS THE PLAYER WILL ALSO BE PENALIZED NO MATTER WHERE THE FLAG IS, IF THEY HIT IT WITH A PUTT FROM ANYWHERE ON THE GREEN.

WHEN YOU ARE ON THE GREEN NEVER, NEVER, NEVER STEP ON THE LINE OF ANOTHER PLAYERS PUTT. YOUR FOOT COULD LEAVE ENOUGH OF AN IMPRESSION IN THE GRASS TO EFFECT THE ROLL OF THAT PLAYERS BALL. IF YOU DO THIS ERROR, KEEP THAT TOWEL HANDY, ESPECIALLY IF YOU CONTINUE TO DO IT.

WHEN YOU ARE ON THE GREEN AND ANOTHER PLAYER IS PUTTING AND YOU ARE NOT HOLDING THE FLAG, KEEP OUT OF THEIR SIGHT AND DO NOT WALK AROUND TRYING TO DETERMINE YOUR ODDS OF MAKING YOUR PUTT. BE COURTEOUS AND WAIT PATIENTLY FOR YOUR TURN.

WHEN IT IS YOUR TURN TO PLAY A GOLF SHOT, BE READY AND GET IT OVER WITH. SLOW PLAYERS ARE HATED BY ALL OTHER GOLFERS AS THEY ARE ABOUT THE MOST IRRITATING THING ON THE GOLF COURSE. YOU WILL UNDERSTAND THIS AS SOON AS YOU GET BEHIND A GROUP OF SNAILS THAT MAKE YOU WAIT 5 - 10 MINUTES BETWEEN EVERY SHOT. YOU WILL WANT TO DO BAD

THINGS TO THEM THEIR FAMILY AND ALL THEIR RELATIVES. IN OTHER WORDS, PLAY YOUR SHOT WITHOUT DELAY.....I.E. MISS IT QUICK.....

KEEP TRACK OF HOW MANY STROKES THAT YOU HAVE TAKEN AT ANY TIME ON A GOLF HOLE. WHEN YOU ARE ASKED AT THE FINISH OF THE HOLE WHAT YOUR SCORE WAS, YOU WILL LOOK PRETTY SILLY TRYING TO ADD YOUR STROKES UP AT THAT TIME, PLUS IT WILL DEFINITELY NOT IMPRESS YOUR PLAYING PARTNERS.

AFTER YOUR GROUP HAS FINISHED PUTTING OUT AND EVERYONE IS DONE FOR THAT HOLE, LEAVE THE GREEN

IMMEDIATELY AND GO DIRECTLY TO THE
NEXT TEEING AREA

WHEN YOUR GROUP HAS FINISHED A
HOLE, DO NOT SIT BESIDE THE GREEN AND
WRITE DOWN YOUR GROUP SCORES. GO TO
THE NEXT HOLE AND THEN DO YOUR
SCORING. IF YOU SIT BESIDE THE GREEN
THE GROUP BEHIND YOU WILL GET VERY
IMPATIENT WAITING TO HIT THEIR
APPROACH SHOTS TO "THEIR" GREEN.
WATCH YOUR HEAD AS I GUARANTEE YOU
THAT ONE OF THEM WILL HIT THE BALL
TOWARDS THE GREEN. THE ONLY PROBLEM
WITH BEING HIT BY A GOLF BALL IS THAT IT
REALLY AND I MEAN REALLY HURTS.

IF AS A RELATIVELY NEW GOLFER YOU ARE UP TO 10 STROKES AND THE GREEN IS STILL JUST A SMALL SPECK IN THE DISTANCE, PICK UP YOUR BALL AND TRY ON THE NEXT HOLE. BELIEVE ME, YOUR PLAYING PARTNERS WILL APPRECIATE THIS COURTESY. AGAIN SLOW PLAY IS NOT WANTED OR TOLERATED ON A GOLF COURSE.

WHEN YOU ARE ON A GREEN AND YOU ARE NOT THE FURTHEST FROM THE HOLE, YOU MUST MARK YOUR GOLF BALL SO THAT IT DOESN'T INTERFERE OR BOTHER ANOTHER PLAYER. THIS IS DONE BY SIMPLY PLACING A COIN DIRECTLY BEHIND YOUR BALL AND REMOVING THE BALL. WHEN IT IS

YOUR TURN TO PLAY, YOU REPLACE THE BALL IN THE EXACT LOCATION THAT YOU MARKED WITH THE COIN AND PROCEED WITH YOUR PUTT. YOU MAY BE ASKED TO MOVE YOUR MARK (COIN) AS IT INTERFERES WITH ANOTHER PLAYERS LINE. TO DO SO SIMPLY LINE YOUR PUTTER UP AT SOME STATIONARY OBJECT IN THE DISTANCE AND MOVE YOUR COIN IN THE DIRECTION FROM ONE SIDE OF THE PUTTER HEAD TO THE SIDE AWAY FROM THE OTHER PLAYERS LINE. YOU MAY HAVE TO MOVE IT TWO PUTTER HEAD LENGTHS AT CERTAIN TIMES. ONCE THE OTHER PLAYER HAS PLAYED YOU MUST REPLACE THE COIN IN ITS ORIGINAL POSITION OR ELSE YOU WILL INCUR A

PENALTY FOR PLAYING A BALL FROM A WRONG POSITION.

WHEN YOU ARE IN THE FAIRWAY AND ANOTHER PLAYER IS ABOUT TO PLAY THEIR SHOT, STOP AND BE QUIET UNTIL THEY HAVE FINISHED. AGAIN IT'S ONLY COURTESY.

THESE ARE JUST A FEW GENERAL COURSE ETIQUETTE ITEMS THAT SHOULD ASSIST A NEW PLAYER ON THE GOLF COURSE.(THERE ARE QUITE A FEW OLD PLAYERS THAT MAY WANT TO PAY ATTENTION TO THIS SECTION ALSO). MOST OF GOLF ETIQUETTE IS SIMPLY GOOD MANNERS AND COMMON SENSE.

CHAPTER 23

ARRIVING AT THE GOLF

COURSE

ARRIVING AT THE GOLF COURSE

WHEN YOU HAVE MADE A TEE TIME TRY AND ARRANGE TO ARRIVE AT THE GOLF COURSE ANYWHERE FROM 20 TO 30 MINUTES BEFORE YOUR SCHEDULED TEE TIME. THIS WILL GIVE YOU SUFFICIENT TIME TO CHECK IN AND HIT A FEW BALLS TO WARM UP PLUS DO SOME PRACTICE PUTTING TO GET READY TO PLAY.

AS YOU ARRIVE AT THE GOLF COURSE YOU MAY HAVE TO GET CLEARED THROUGH A SECURITY GATE. NORMALLY A GUARD WILL ASK YOU THE PURPOSE OF YOUR VISIT

AND WHEN YOU TELL HIM YOUR RESERVED TEE TIME HE WILL VERIFY IT AND GIVE YOU A DAY PASS AND LET YOU PROCEED ONTO THE GOLF COURSE PROPERTY.

ONCE ON GOLF COURSE PROPERTY OBEY ALL SPEED LIMIT SIGNS AS THEY ARE THERE FOR THE PROTECTION OF THE MEMBERS AND VISITING PLAYERS.

WHEN YOU ARRIVE AT THE CLUB HOUSE YOU WILL SEE A BAG DROP SIGN. YOU CAN DRIVE UP TO IT AND ONE OF THE ASSISTANTS WILL REMOVE YOUR CLUBS FROM YOUR TRUNK FOR YOU, OR YOU CAN GO DIRECTLY TO THE PARKING LOT AND CARRY YOUR CLUBS TO THE STARTERS

AREA WHERE AN ASSISTANT WILL THEN TAKE THEM AND ASK YOU FOR YOUR TEE TIME. THE ASSISTANT WILL PUT YOUR CLUBS ON A GOLF CART.

IT IS A NORMAL AND ACCEPTED PRACTICE TO TIP THESE ASSISTANTS AS TIPS ARE A MAJORITY OF THEIR EARNINGS. USUALLY A COUPLE OF DOLLARS WILL BRING A SMILE AND A THANK YOU. IF YOU WANT YOUR SHOES SHINED, A BACK RUB AND FULL MASSAGE, TIP THEM 5 OR 10 DOLLARS.(JUST KIDDING)

NOW YOU NEED TO ENTER THE PRO SHOP TO SIGN IN AND PAY FOR THE EXPERIENCE YOU ARE ABOUT TO ENJOY.

THE PRO SHOP WILL NORMALLY GIVE YOU A STARTERS TICKET (RECEIPT) THAT YOU WILL NEED TO SHOW TO THE STARTER BEFORE YOU BEGIN PLAY.

ONCE YOU HAVE FINISHED IN THE PRO SHOP YOU CAN GO TO THE GOLF CART THAT HAS YOUR BAG ON IT AND PROCEED TO THE PRACTICE RANGE TO WARM UP. MOST CLASSY GOLF COURSES HAVE BALLS ON THE RANGE FOR YOU TO USE BUT SOME WILL FORCE YOU TO PURCHASE A BUCKET OF RANGE BALLS TO WARM UP WITH.

NOTE THAT ONCE YOU HAVE PAID YOUR GREEN FEES YOU ARE ACTUALLY A MEMBER OF THAT CLUB FOR THE TIME THAT

YOU ARE THERE. YOU CAN USE ALL THEIR PRACTICE FACILITIES SUCH AS THE RANGE, CHIPPING AREA, SAND BUNKER PRACTICE AREA AND THEIR PUTTING GREEN PRIOR TO YOUR ROUND OF GOLF. AFTER YOUR ROUND YOU CAN VISIT THEIR BAR AND DINING AREAS.

AT SOME POINT AFTER YOUR ARRIVAL THE COURSE STARTER WILL APPROACH YOU FOR YOUR TEE TIME. HE/SHE WILL ADVISE YOU WHEN YOU ARE TO GO TO THE FIRST HOLE. WHEN YOU APPROACH THE FIRST HOLE AND THE GROUP IN FRONT OF YOU HAS NOT LEFT THE TEE AREA, STAY BACK AND OUT OF COURTESY WAIT FOR THEM TO LEAVE BEFORE YOU APPROACH THE TEE OFF AREA.

AFTER YOU HAVE FINISHED YOUR ROUND OF GOLF THE ASSISTANTS WILL CLEAN YOUR CLUBS AND PLACE THEM ON THE OUT GOING BAG RACK FOR YOU. AGAIN A TIP IS ACCEPTABLE AND HIGHLY APPRECIATED.

HOPEFULLY YOU HAVE HAD A FUN DAY AND WILL RETURN AGAIN TO TRY AND MASTER THIS PARTICULAR GOLF COURSE.

CHAPTER 24

GOLF WORDS AND THEIR

MEANINGS

GOLF WORDS AND THEIR MEANINGS

HERE ARE A FEW EXAMPLES THAT SHOULD ASSIST NEW GOLFERS IN BECOMING FAMILIAR WITH SOME OF GOLFS TERMS.

FORWARD: MEANS TOWARD THE HOLE OR GOLF TARGET. IF YOU ARE RIGHT HANDED AND YOU TAKE YOUR STANCE FORWARD IS TOWARDS THE LEFT SIDE OF YOUR BODY. (THE OPPOSITE FOR YOU LEFTIES)

BACK: MEANS JUST THE OPPOSITE OF FORWARD. I.E. TOWARDS YOUR RIGHT SIDE. (AGAIN LEFTIES, YOU KNOW THE DIFFERENCE)

BALL POSITION: REFERS TO THE PLACEMENT OF THE GOLF BALL IN YOUR STANCE. IF IT IS CLOSER TO YOUR LEFT SIDE FOR RIGHT HANDED GOLFERS IT IS CONSIDERED FORWARD IN THEIR STANCE.

LIE: THIS DOES NOT REFER TO THE SCORE THAT YOU PUT DOWN ON YOUR SCORE CARD. IT REFERS TO HOW THE GOLF BALL IS POSITIONED ON THE GROUND. IF THE BALL IS SITTING UP ON TOP OF THE GRASS IT WOULD BE CONSIDERED A GOOD

LIE. IF IT WERE DOWN IN THE GRASS IT WOULD BE A BAD LIE.

STANCE: THIS REFERS TO YOUR POSITION ONCE YOU ARE READY TO HIT THE GOLF BALL. WHEN YOU APPROACH THE GOLF BALL AND TAKE YOUR ATHLETIC POSITION OVER THE BALL, YOU HAVE ASSUMED A STANCE.

CHOKE DOWN: WHEN YOU LOWER YOUR HANDS ON THE GRIP OF THE GOLF CLUB. THE MORE YOU CHOKE DOWN ON THE SHAFT THE MORE OF IT WILL BE STICKING ABOVE YOUR GRIP.

YOU'RE AWAY: MEANS THAT YOUR GOLF BALL IS THE FURTHEST AWAY FROM THE HOLE AND IT IS YOUR TURN TO PLAY. THIS TERM IS NORMALLY USED ON THE GREEN.

YOU'RE STILL AWAY: THIS YOU NEVER WANT TO HEAR. IT'S ALMOST LIKE A WOMAN TELLING YOU THAT SHE LOVES YOU BUT SHE'S NOT IN LOVE WITH YOU. BOTH CAN BE AS DEVASTATING.

OPEN: NORMALLY MEANS THAT THE SUBJECT BEING DISCUSSED IS AIMING TOO FAR LEFT OF THE TARGET (LEFTIES AGAIN IT IS OPPOSITE) IT CAN BE YOUR CLUB YOUR STANCE ETC..

CLOSED: MEANS THE SUBJECT IS AIMED TOO FAR TO THE RIGHT.

PENALTY STROKE: MEANS THAT YOU HAVE EITHER BROKEN A RULE OR THAT THE POSITION OF THE GOLF BALL IS SUCH THAT YOU MUST TAKE RELIEF IN ORDER TO HIT IT. BE CAREFUL AS THERE ARE CERTAIN CIRCUMSTANCES WHERE YOU GET RELIEF WITHOUT TAKING A PENALTY. REFER TO THE RULE BOOK.

RELIEF: DOESN'T MEAN THAT THE ROUND IS FINALLY OVER, IT SIMPLY MEANS THAT UNDER THE RULES OF GOLF YOU GET RELIEF (I.E. YOU GET TO MOVE THE BALL) FROM THE POSITION YOUR BALL IS IN.

Cec McFarlane

CHECK THE RULES TO SEE IF A PENALTY IS REQUIRED FOR THE RELIEF SITUATION YOU ARE IN.

PROVISIONAL BALL: IF YOU HIT A BALL THAT YOU BELIEVE IS GOING TO BE LOST OR OUT OF BOUNDS YOU MAY HIT A SECOND BALL AFTER ANNOUNCING THAT YOU ARE GOING TO HIT A PROVISIONAL BALL. IF YOUR FIRST BALL IS FOUND YOU PLAY IT (PROVIDED IT IS NOT OUT OF BOUNDS) . IF THE FIRST BALL IS NOT FOUND OR IS ACTUALLY OUT OF BOUNDS, YOU PLAY YOUR PROVISIONAL BALL INCURRING A STROKE PENALTY. I.E. YOUR FIRST SWING PLUS THE PENALTY...YOUR PROVISIONAL IS YOUR THIRD SWING...THUS YOU LAY 3)

HOLING OUT: SIMPLY MEANS FINISHING THE GOLF HOLE BY PUTTING THE BALL IN THE GOLF HOLE (CUP)

LINE OF PUTT: REFERS TO A STRAIGHT LINE FROM YOUR BALL TO THE GOLF HOLE.

LINE OF PLAY: REFERS TO A STRAIGHT LINE FROM ANYWHERE ON THE GOLF COURSE FROM YOUR BALL TO THE HOLE.

HAZZARD: REFERS TO AN AREA DESIGNATED BY THE GOLF COURSE. IT CAN BE A WATER HAZZARD OR ANY OTHER FORM OF HAZZARD THAT IS DECIDED UPON BY THE COURSE . READ THE RULE BOOK ON

HAZZARDS TO DETERMINE PENALTIES AND OPTIONS ASSOCIATED WITH THE VARIOUS FORMS OF HAZZARDS.

TENDING THE FLAG: WHEN YOU ARE ON THE GREEN YOU MAY BE ASKED TO TEND THE FLAG FOR ANOTHER PLAYER. IT SIMPLY MEANS FOR YOU TO HOLD THE FLAG IN THE HOLE UNTIL THE OTHER PLAYER HAS MADE THEIR STROKE AND THEN YOU REMOVE IT (QUICKLY, IF YOU WANT TO TAKE HOME ALL THE BODY PARTS YOU STARTED WITH) SO THAT THE PLAYER DOES NOT RECEIVE A PENALTY BY THEIR BALL STRIKING THE FLAG WHEN THEY HAVE MADE A PUTTING STROKE WHILE ON THE GREEN.

FORE: MEANS DUCK AND GET YOUR HANDS COVERING YOUR FACE AS SOME OTHER PLAYER HAS JUST HIT A BALL THAT IS COMING IN YOUR DIRECTION.

JERK: THAT'S WHAT YOU YELL BACK AT THE MORON WHO JUST ABOUT TOOK YOUR HEAD OFF . (JUST KIDDING, AS GOLF IS A GAME RESERVED FOR GENTLEMEN.........UTTER IT UNDER YOUR BREATH)

THERE ARE MANY MORE WORDS AND SAYINGS BUT THESE SHOULD BE SUFFICIENT FOR NEW GOLFERS TO SOUND AS IF THEY ACTUALLY HAVE AN IDEA OF WHERE THEY ARE.

CHAPTER 25

SCORE CARDS

<u>SCORE CARDS</u>

A GREAT MANY NEW GOLFERS HAVE A DIFFICULT TIME UNDERSTANDING A SCORE CARD AND THE INFORMATION IT CONTAINS.

MOST SCORE CARDS FOLLOW A VERY SIMILAR DESIGN. THEY ARE TWO SIDED AND THE WAY THAT THEY ARE FOLDED ALLOWS PLAYERS TO SEE THEIR NAMES ON BOTH THE FRONT AND BACK NINES. THIS IS DONE TO FACILITATE THE EASE OF KEEPING SCORE.

THE FRONT OF THE SCORE CARD IS USUALLY RESERVED FOR THE GOLF COURSE NAME AND LOGO.

WHEN YOU OPEN UP THE CARD, THE LEFT HAND SIDE (USUALLY 3/4 OF THE COMPLETE SIDE) HAS INFORMATION ABOUT THE FRONT NINE HOLES.

THE IMMEDIATE LEFT PORTION USUALLY HAS THE WORD HOLE AND UNDERNEATH IT ARE LISTED VARIOUS COLOR NAMES. THESE SIGNIFY THE DIFFERENT TEE OPTIONS AVAILABLE TO BE PLAYED FROM. THE FIRST COLOR SHOWN IS NORMALLY THE CHAMPIONSHIP (PROFESSIONAL) TEE AND THE BOTTOM ONE IS NORMALLY THE

SENIOR TEE. IN BETWEEN THESE ARE USUALLY COLORS FOR MEMBERS (LONG) MEMBERS (REGULAR) AND LADIES TEES.

DIRECTLY TO THE RIGHT OF THESE COLORS AND UNDERNEATH THE INDIVIDUAL HOLE NUMBERS ARE NUMBERS THAT TELL THE LENGTH OF EACH HOLE IN YARDS, FOR EACH INDIVIDUAL TEE COLOR. THE DISTANCES SHOWN ARE USUALLY THE DISTANCE FROM THE TEE IN CONCERN TO THE CENTER OF THE GREEN, AS THE CROW FLIES. YOU WILL SEE A LARGE DIFFERENCE BETWEEN THE DISTANCE OF THE PRO TEES TO THAT OF THE OTHER TEES. THIS IS DONE TO EQUAL OUT THE GOLF COURSE SO THAT ALL CALIBER AND AGES OF PLAYERS HAVE

Cec McFarlane

A FAIR CHANCE TO PLAY THE COURSE ON FAIRLY EQUAL TERMS.

TO THE RIGHT OF THE LISTED HOLES YOU WILL NORMALLY SEE THE WORD OUT. THIS IS SIMPLY THAT THE FRONT NINE GOES AWAY FROM THE CLUB HOUSE OR OUT TOWARDS THE REST OF THE COURSE.

BELOW ALL THIS INFORMATION YOU WILL SEE BLANK SPACES THAT ARE THERE TO RECORD THE PLAYER'S NAMES AND THEIR SCORES FOR EACH HOLE.

UNDER THIS THERE IS USUALLY A LINE THAT READS PAR WITH A DIFFERENT NUMBER UNDER EACH HOLE. THIS SIMPLY

TELLS YOU THE PAR RATING FOR EACH HOLE DIRECTLY ABOVE THE NUMBER.

BELOW THIS IS USUALLY A LINE THAT READS HANDICAP WITH DIFFERENT NUMBERS UNDER EACH HOLE. THIS IS SIMPLY THE DIFFICULTY RATING FOR EACH HOLE. FOR EXAMPLE IF HOLE 3 HAS A HANDICAP RATING OF 7, IT IS RATED AS THE 7TH MOST DIFFICULT HOLE ON THE GOLF COURSE. IF YOU WERE A 23 HANDICAPPED PLAYER AND YOU WERE PLAYING A MATCH AGAINST A 30 HANDICAP PLAYER, YOU WOULD HAVE TO GIVE THAT PLAYER A STROKE ON THE 7 HARDEST HOLES ON THE GOLF COURSE. THE BALANCE OF THE HOLES WOULD BE PLAYED ON AN EVEN

BASIS. THIS METHOD IS USED IN AN ATTEMPT TO EQUAL THE COURSE SCORING FOR EVERYONE.

NORMALLY ON THE RIGHT HAND SIDE OF THIS PAGE IS INFORMATION SUCH AS COURSE RULES, REGULATIONS ETC. IT MAY EVEN CONTAIN A SECTION THAT SAYS DATE, SCORER AND THE WORD ATTEST. IF YOU WERE PLAYING IN A TOURNAMENT ANOTHER PLAYER WOULD KEEP YOUR SCORE SO THEIR NAME WOULD GO IN THE SECTION OF SCORER. YOU AS THE PLAYER WOULD HAVE TO ATTEST THAT THE SCORE THEY ENTERED IS YOUR ACTUAL SCORE. IF THE SCORER MADE A MISTAKE AND YOU

ATTEST TO IT YOU WILL BE PENALIZED,
USUALLY BY BEING DISQUALIFIED.

ON THE LEFT THIRD OF THE BACK SIDE
OF THE CARD YOU USUALLY HAVE THE
INFORMATION ABOUT THE BACK OR IN NINE
HOLES. WHEN YOU FINISH YOUR ROUND
THE FRONT NINE SCORES AND BACK NINE
SCORES ARE ADDED TO OBTAIN YOUR
TOTAL SCORE FOR 18 HOLES.

YOU WILL ALSO SEE THE LETTERS HCP
AND THIS IS FOR THE INDIVIDUAL HANDICAP
THAT YOU HAVE OR CARRY. YOU WILL ALSO
SEE THE WORD NET WHICH IS ARRIVED AT
BY TAKING YOUR ACTUAL SCORE AND
SUBTRACTING YOUR HANDICAP FROM IT.

EXAMPLE: IF WHEN YOU ADD UP YOUR TOTAL SCORE YOU COME TO A TOTAL OF 95. YOU ENTER THAT NUMBER UNDER TOTAL AND LETS SAY YOU ARE A 22 HANDICAP PLAYER, YOU ENTER 22 IN THE HCP SECTION AND THEN SUBTRACT THAT AMOUNT FROM THE TOTAL OF 95 TO REACH A NET SCORE OF 73 OR 1 OVER PAR. THIS HANDICAP SYSTEM IS SET UP TO ALLOW VARYING SKILLED PLAYERS TO COMPETE ON AN EQUAL BASIS AGAINST EACH OTHER.

YOU OBTAIN A HANDICAP BY SUBMITTING ALL YOUR SCORES TO YOUR CLUB PRO OR BY ENTERING THEM INTO THE PRO SHOPS COMPUTER AND A STANDARD METHOD IS

USED TO DETERMINE EACH GOLFERS HANDICAP.

YOU SHOULD ALSO SEE SUCH INFORMATION ON THE SCORE CARD AS SLOPE AND RATING. THIS INFORMATION IS USED TO EQUAL VARIOUS COURSES AND ALLOWS YOUR CLUB PRO TO DETERMINE YOUR HANDICAP. USUALLY THE HIGHER THE SLOPE RATING THE TOUGHER THE GOLF COURSE. THE RATING NUMBER SIMPLY SHOWS WHAT YOUR COURSE HAS BEEN RATED AT FOR THE INDIVIDUAL TEE DISTANCES AS COMPARED TO A NATIONAL AVERAGE. IF YOUR COURSE WERE RATED AT A 73.4 FOR THE BLUE TEES, IT WOULD SIMPLY MEAN THAT IF A 22 HANDICAPPED

GOLFER WERE TO PLAY YOUR COURSE FROM THE BLUE TEES THEIR EXPECTED SCORE AFTER THEIR HANDICAP WOULD BE 1.4 STROKES MORE THAN AVERAGE. THAT IS BECAUSE THIS COURSE IS RATED HARDER THAN THEIR NORMAL ONE. THE RATINGS CAN ALSO BE LOWER THAN YOUR HOME COURSE. ALL OF THIS IS DONE TO AGAIN TRY AND EQUAL THE PLAYING FIELD SO THAT ALL GOLFERS CAN COMPETE ON FAIRLY EQUAL TERMS.

SOME OTHER INFORMATION THAT IS USUALLY FOUND ON THE SCORE CARD IS THE NAME OF THE COURSE DESIGNER, THE HEAD PROFESSIONAL AND THE GREENS KEEPER.

WHENEVER YOU PLAY A NEW COURSE, READ THEIR SCORE CARD AS SOME OF THEIR LOCAL RULES MAY SAVE YOU A FEW STROKES, SHOULD YOU GET INTO TROUBLE.

PUT IN HONEST GOLF SCORES TO OBTAIN AN HONEST HANDICAP. ONCE YOU HAVE ESTABLISHED A HANDICAP YOUR GOAL IS TO GET IT AS LOW AS POSSIBLE, THUS SHOWING AN IMPROVEMENT IN YOUR GOLFING ABILITIES.

CHAPTER 26

SWING TRAINING AIDS

SWING TRAINING AIDS

MOST SWING TRAINING AIDS (OR GIMMICKS) ARE ABOUT AS USEFUL AS THOSE X-RAY GLASSES YOU PURCHASED OFF THE BACK OF A COMIC BOOK WHEN YOU WERE 12 YEARS OLD.

ALTHOUGH SOME OF THEM GIVE YOU A FEEL FOR CERTAIN PARTS OF THE GOLF SWING, I HAVE NEVER SEEN ONE THAT DOES THE COMPLETE SWING.

MOST OF THE GIMMICKS FORCE YOU INTO A SWING THAT YOU WILL NOT BE ABLE

TO DO WITHOUT IT. REMEMBER, YOUR SWING IS UNIQUE TO YOU AND YOU ALONE. YOU ARE NEVER GOING TO SWING LIKE TIGER WOODS OR ANY OTHER PROFESSIONAL.

HOWEVER, IF THE GIMMICK THAT YOU JUST COMMITTED 3 EASY PAYMENTS OF $49 FOR HAS SOMEHOW BEEN MODELED AFTER YOUR INDIVIDUAL SWING, YOU HAVE JUST MADE A WISE INVESTMENT. IF IT HAS NOT BEEN.....WELL!...

YOU WOULD DO YOUR GOLF SWING AND GOLF GAME A FAR BETTER JUSTICE BY SPENDING YOUR MONEY ON SOMETHING PRODUCTIVE, SUCH AS A SERIES OF

PRIVATE LESSONS. AH, REALITY....WHAT A CONCEPT.

CHAPTER 27

CONTROLLING THE

MENTAL GAME

<u>CONTROLLING THE MENTAL GAME</u>

ONE OF THE MOST DIFFICULT PARTS OF PLAYING GOOD SOLID GOLF IS CONTROLLING YOUR MIND. FOR EXAMPLE: HOW MANY TIMES HAVE YOU BEEN ON THE FIRST TEE AND FELT THAT SPECIAL YUCKY TURNING OF YOUR STOMACH. YOU THEN PROCEED TO DRIBBLE THE BALL OFF THE TEE, IF YOU HAPPEN TO ACTUALLY MAKE CONTACT. THIS IS ALL CAUSED BY YOUR MIND AND NERVES THAT ARE VERY COMMON TO ALL GOLFERS. CONTROLLING THESE NERVES IS A REQUIREMENT IF YOU EVER EXPECT TO PLAY WELL.

TRY THIS THE NEXT TIME YOU ARE ON THE FIRST TEE. BEFORE YOU TEE OFF TAKE 3 OR 4 DEEP BREATHS AND DON'T TRY TO HIT THE PERFECT GOLF SHOT. TRUST THE SWING THAT YOU HAVE WORKED SO HARD TO DEVELOP AND TRY TO HIT THE BALL ABOUT 3/4 OF THE DISTANCE THAT YOU NORMALLY DO. YOU MAY BE SURPRISED AT HOW WELL YOU ACTUALLY STRIKE THE BALL.

A LOT OF AMATEURS ARE CONCERNED THAT THEY MAKE A PERFECT SWING AND THAT THEY WANT TO IMPRESS THEIR FELLOW GOLFERS OR THEY ARE WORRIED THAT THEIR FELLOW GOLFERS WILL THINK

NEGATIVE THOUGHTS ABOUT YOUR GOLFING ABILITY.. TRY AND REMEMBER THAT THE MAJORITY OF OTHER GOLFERS ARE SO TIED UP IN HAVING THE SAME THOUGHTS THAT YOU DO THAT ALL THEY WANT IS FOR YOU TO MAKE YOUR SWING AND GET TO HELL OFF THE TEE SO THEY CAN HAVE THEIR TURN. THEY COULDN'T CARE LESS ABOUT YOUR POSTURE, ABILITY OR RESULTS. IF THEY DON'T CARE WHY SHOULD YOU BE SO CONCERNED ABOUT HOW THEY THINK.

AFTER YOUR INITIAL TEE SHOT AND HOPEFULLY IT IS SOMEWHERE DOWN THE FAIRWAY, TAKE ONE EXTRA CLUB FOR YOUR APPROACH SHOT TO THE GREEN AS

YOUR NERVES AND DESIRE TO SUCCEED WITH BE AT THEIR HIGHEST ON THE VERY FIRST HOLE. TRY AND MAKE THE BEST SWING THAT YOU CAN AND ACCEPT WHATEVER FATE THE GOLF GODS HAVE IN STORE FOR YOU TODAY . IF YOU HAPPEN TO HIT A BAD SHOT, REMIND YOURSELF THAT YOU HAVE HIT WORSE SHOTS, YOU MAY NOT BE ABLE TO REMEMBER WHEN, BUT YOU MUST HAVE.

IF YOU DO MAKE A BAD SHOT, DON'T GET ANGRY AT YOURSELF. IF YOU ARE LIKE MOST PEOPLE, YOU HAVE ENOUGH PEOPLE ANGRY AT YOU, SO WHY GET ANGRY AT YOURSELF.

IF YOU HAVE A TENDENCY TO THROW A CLUB, BEFORE YOU DO SO, CONSIDER JUST HOW TOTALLY STUPID IT LOOKS AND HOW ANY RESPECT THAT THE OTHER PLAYERS HAD FOR YOU IS NOW RELEGATED TO THAT OF A SPOILED LITTLE CHILD. IF YOU REACT IN THIS MANNER TO A SILLY GOLF SHOT THINK OF HOW OTHER PEOPLE MUST THINK OF HOW YOU WOULD REACT TO A REAL CRISIS. RESPECT CAN TURN TO PITY AFTER OTHERS SEE YOUR UNCONTROLLED ANGER.

IF YOU MAKE A BAD SHOT AND YOU FEEL UPSET OR ANGRY, LEAVE THE GOLF COURSE AND STOP THE FIRST 20 OR 30 CARS GOING BY ON THE HIGHWAY, TELL

THEM THAT YOU HAVE JUST MADE A BAD GOLF SHOT AND SEE IF THEY GIVE A DARN. IF THEY DON'T CARE, WHY SHOULD YOU.

IF YOU TEND TO GET ANGRY AND LOSE CONTROL ON THE GOLF COURSE, I HAVE AN OFFER THAT YOU CAN'T RESIST. INSTEAD OF SPENDING THE MONEY FOR A ROUND OF GOLF, SEND ME HALF OF IT AND I WILL LET YOU ABUSE YOURSELF TO YOUR HEARTS CONTENT. IT WILL SAVE YOU A TON PLUS LET YOU BE A BABY IN THE PRIVACY OF YOUR OWN HOME.

SOMETHING THAT YOU SHOULD CONSIDER IS THAT WHEN YOU SHOW ANGER ON A GOLF COURSE, YOU NOT ONLY

RUIN YOUR OWN GAME YOU EFFECT THAT OF THE PEOPLE PLAYING WITH YOU. THEY BECOME VERY NERVOUS AS TO WHEN YOUR NEXT TANTRUM WILL OCCUR PLUS THEY WILL QUICKLY LOOK TO AVOID PLAYING WITH YOU IN THE FUTURE.

YOUR EMOTIONS CONTROL A VERY LARGE PART OF YOUR GOLF GAME AND IF YOU CANNOT CONTROL THEM WHILE YOU ARE ON THE COURSE, YOU MAY WANT TO THINK OF ANOTHER GAME TO TAKE UP. IF YOU ARE AGITATED YOU WILL NOT BE ABLE TO THINK RATIONALLY NOR WILL YOU BE ABLE TO MAKE A NICE SMOOTH GOLF SWING.

WHEN YOU ARE PLAYING TRY AND VISUALIZE EVERY SHOT BEFORE YOU ACTUALLY SWING. PICTURE THE FLIGHT OF THE BALL AND IMAGINE HOW AND WHERE IT WILL LAND. YOU WILL BE AMAZED AT HOW THIS WILL HELP YOUR SCORING.

WHEN A FELLOW PLAYER MAKES A GOOD SHOT BE PLEASED FOR THEM AND DON'T FEEL THAT YOU MUST MAKE AN EQUALLY PERFECT SHOT. YOU WILL BE MORE SUCCESSFUL IF YOU PLAY TO YOUR GAME AND NOT SOME OTHER PLAYERS.

LEARN AND ACCEPT YOUR OWN ABILITIES OR LACK THERE OF. IF YOU HAVE A 200 YARD SHOT THAT IS ALL CARRY TO A

PROTECTED GREEN SURROUNDED BY TROUBLE AND YOU KNOW IN YOUR GUT THAT YOU WILL HAVE TO HIT THE BEST SHOT OF YOUR LIFE TO ACCOMPLISH IT, DON'T TRY IT. INSTEAD HIT A SHOT THAT YOU KNOW YOU CAN DO. PLAYING SMART GOLF USUALLY GIVES YOU A BOGEY AT WORSE, PLAYING MACHO OR STUPID GOLF CAN INCREASE THESE NUMBERS VERY QUICKLY AND THEN OF ALL THE SILLY THINGS, YOU WILL MOST LIKELY GET UPSET WITH YOURSELF.....WHAT'S WRONG WITH THIS PICTURE?.

GOLF IS JUST A GAME, IT IS REALLY NOT THAT IMPORTANT, YET HOW YOU PLAY IT AND HOW YOU REACT TELLS PEOPLE A LOT

ABOUT YOUR CHARACTER AND YOUR MATURITY.

IF YOU WANT TO HAVE MORE FUN PLAYING GOLF ACCEPT THAT YOU OR NO ONE ELSE WILL EVER HIT EVERY SHOT PERFECT. IF YOU HIT A BAD SHOT, THAT JUST GIVES YOU THE OPPORTUNITY TO TRY AGAIN. KEEP THIS GAME LIGHT AND YOUR SCORES WILL REACT ACCORDINGLY.

YOU CAN TELL MORE ABOUT A PERSON IN A ROUND OF GOLF THAN YOU EVER CAN IN YEARS OF DEALING WITH THEM. THE NEXT TIME YOU GET ANGRY ON A GOLF COURSE, DON'T BE SURPRISED IF ONE OF

YOUR FELLOW PLAYERS OFFERS YOU SOME

CHEESE TO GO WITH THAT WHINE..

Cec McFarlane

ABOUT THE AUTHOR

THE AUTHOR OF "THROW IT DON'T HIT IT" IS A VERY WELL KNOWN AND SOUGHT AFTER GOLF TEACHING SPECIALIST IN SOUTH WEST FLORIDA.

FOR YEARS HIS UNIQUE, GOLF IS EASY - WHEN YOU KNOW HOW, METHOD OF TEACHING HAS ASSISTED THOUSANDS OF GOLFERS TO IMPROVE THEIR GOLF GAME. BOTH AMATEUR AND PROFESSIONAL GOLFERS AS WELL AS A LARGE INTERNATIONAL STUDENT BASE ARE LOYAL STUDENTS TO CEC AND HIS NO SMOKE AND MIRRORS MANNER OF TEACHING.

HIS SUCCESS RATE AT IMPROVING GOLFERS IS RATHER IMPRESSIVE. DURING THE PAST COUPLE OF YEARS HE HAS TAKEN A 32 HANDICAPPED GOLFER DOWN

TO A 12, A 19 HANDICAP DOWN TO A 7, AND A 6 DOWN TO SCRATCH. THIS IS JUST A SMALL SAMPLING OF HIS SUCCESS IN TEACHING STUDENTS THE SIMPLICITY OF THE GAME.

HE TRULY BELIEVES THAT BAD GOLFERS ARE CAUSED BY A LACK OF BASIC UNDERSTANDING OF THE PHYSICS OF THE GAME AND HOW INCORRECT ANGLES EFFECT A GOLFERS ABILITY TO DO A CORRECT GOLF SWING.

ONCE YOU HAVE READ "THROW IT DON'T HIT IT" YOU WILL REALIZE WHY CEC IS SO MUCH IN DEMAND AS A GOLF TEACHING SPECIALIST.